IMAGES OF ASIA

Mandarin Squares
Mandarins and their Insignia

Titles in the series

At the Chinese Table
T.C. LAI

Balinese Paintings
(Second Edition)
A.A.M. DJELANTIK

The Birds of Java and Bali
DEREK HOLMES AND
STEVEN NASH

The Chinese House: Craft,
Symbol, and the Folk Tradition
RONALD G. KNAPP

Chinese Jade
JOAN HARTMAN-GOLDSMITH

Folk Pottery in South-East Asia
DAWN F. ROONEY

Fruits of South-East Asia:
Facts and Folklore
JACQUELINE M. PIPER

A Garden of Eden: Plant Life in
South-East Asia
WENDY VEEVERS-CARTER

The House in South-East Asia
JACQUES DUMARÇAY

Images of the Buddha
in Thailand
DOROTHY H. FICKLE

Indonesian Batik: Processes,
Patterns and Places
SYLVIA FRASER-LU

Japanese Cinema: An Introduction
DONALD RICHIE

The Kris: Mystic Weapon of the
Malay World (Second Edition)
EDWARD FREY

Life in the Javanese Kraton
AART VAN BEEK

Macau
CESAR GUILLEN-NUÑEZ

Mandarin Squares:
Mandarins and their Insignia
VALERY M. GARRETT

Musical Instruments of
South-East Asia
ERIC TAYLOR

Old Bangkok
MICHAEL SMITHIES

Riches of the Wild: Land Mammals
of South-East Asia
EARL OF CRANBROOK

Sarawak Crafts: Methods,
Materials, and Motifs
HEIDI MUNAN

Silverware of South-East Asia
SYLVIA FRASER-LU

Traditional Chinese Clothing in
Hong Kong and South China,
1840 – 1980
VALERY M. GARRETT

Series Editors, China Titles
NIGEL CAMERON, SYLVIA FRASER-LU

Mandarin Squares
Mandarins and their Insignia

VALERY M. GARRETT

HONG KONG
OXFORD UNIVERSITY PRESS
OXFORD   NEW YORK
1990

Oxford University Press

Oxford   New York   Toronto
Petaling Jaya   Singapore   Hong Kong   Tokyo
Delhi   Bombay   Calcutta   Madras   Karachi
Nairobi   Dar es Salaam   Cape Town
Melbourne   Auckland

and associated companies in
Berlin   Ibadan

First published 1990
Published in the United States
by Oxford University Press, Inc., New York

Library of Congress Cataloging-in-Publication Data

Garrett, Valery M., 1942 –
Mandarin Squares: Mandarins and their insignia/Valery M. Garrett.
p. cm. — (Images of Asia)
Includes bibliographical references and index.
ISBN 0-19-585239-7
1. China — Politics and government — 1644 – 1912.   2. Manchus — Costume.
3. Insignia — China.   I. Title.   II. Series.
JQ 1508 . G37 1990
951 .03 — dc20   90-48470
CIP
British Library Cataloguing in Publication Data
available

Printed in Hong Kong by Nordica Printing Co., Ltd.
Published by Oxford University Press, Warwick House, Hong Kong

To the memory of my parents
George and Emily Hayes

Contents

	Preface	*vii*
1	Introduction	1
2	The Imperial Examinations	3
3	The Role of the Mandarin	11
4	The Dress of the Mandarin	19
5	The Development of Mandarin Squares	33
6	Civil Squares	40
7	Military Squares	43
8	Symbolism Used on the Rank Badges	46
9	Methods of Making the Badges	53
	Conclusion	59
	Glossary	60
	Appendix	61
	Bibliography	62
	Index	64

Preface

IN 1644 the invading Manchu army, advancing from beyond the north-eastern frontier of China, overthrew the ruling Ming dynasty led by the Chinese Qongzhen emperor and took control of the country. The Manchus imposed their culture on the local population and established their own imprint on the existing government. The system, administered by a large body of officials known to the West as mandarins, continued throughout the dynasty until the overthrow of the government and the founding of the Republic of China in 1912. The first part of this book gives an introduction to the way men were selected to become mandarins, their attire, and their duties once they had reached this position of great importance.

Badges of rank, or mandarin squares as they are often referred to, are one of the main emblems left from that form of government. These embroidered insignia, about thirty centimetres square, were sewn to front and back of the mandarin's robe, and indicated the status of the wearer. Examples of these fine pieces of embroidery appear from time to time in antique shops and auction sales around the world. The second half of this book traces the origin and development of the squares, and assists in the identification of them.

All Chinese terms, including names of people and places, have been rendered in the *pinyin* romanization.

Several people gave me helpful advice and information. In particular I should like to mention the support and enthusiasm once again forthcoming from Dr James Hayes. I am most grateful for his knowledge of the local and provincial system of government. He also kindly took the time and trouble to read my manuscript.

No book on rank badges could have been attempted without recourse to the pioneering work begun by Dr Schuyler Cammann in the 1940s. Thanks are also due to Teresa Coleman, Judith Rutherford, Chris Hall, and Stephen McGuinness for sharing their knowledge of insignia badges. Finally, last but by no means least, thanks must go to Helen Perrell who first drew my attention to the pursuit of this intriguing and rewarding collection some fifteen years ago.

Hong Kong, 1990   VALERY M. GARRETT

I
Introduction

F R O M very early times China had been subjected to attacks from neighbouring invaders. During the reign of Qinshi Huangdi (First Emperor of the Qin) (221–206 BC) a series of walls were linked together to form the Great Wall, in an attempt to protect the agricultural central plains from the marauding and barbaric nomads who lived on the steppes to the north and west. But throughout successive dynasties, groups of invaders continually threatened the Chinese state and in 1644 one such group succeeded in overthrowing the reigning Ming dynasty. These conquering people were called the Manchus, formerly a nomadic tribe of Tungus origin from the region beyond the northern frontier of China now called Manchuria.

In earlier centuries their livelihood had depended on hunting and fishing, but as time went on they developed an agrarian civilization similar to that already existing in China. They traded sable furs and ginseng with the army of the reigning Ming dynasty along Liaodong peninsula, and the Ming bribed the Manchus with dragon robes and tribute silk as well as titles and favours in an attempt to control the tribesmen. Continuing fighting among the tribes made Nurhachu from the Aisin Gioro clan the head of the numerous clans. Given the title of brigadier by the Ming he became supreme chieftain of all Tungusic tribes in Manchuria. By the time of his death in 1626, he had driven the Ming forces out of the Liaodong peninsula.

His successor Abahai formally took the name Manchu for the collective tribes and named the new dynasty Qing, meaning 'pure'. After Abahai's death in 1643 his younger brother Dorgon continued his rule, acting as regent for his young son Shunzhi. At this time a rebel leader Li Zicheng captured Beijing (Peking) and the Ming emperor committed suicide. The Ming border troops at the Great Wall returned to Beijing to defend it, and Dorgon bribed the defending general Wu Sangui with a princely title and promised to punish the rebels. General Wu allowed the Manchus through the Great Wall and Dorgon and his army entered Beijing on 1 June 1644, setting up his nephew Shunzhi as the first Manchu emperor.

Comprising only 2 per cent of the total population of their empire, the Manchus' immediate concern was to preserve their own identity as well as their special status. Apart from the imperial family, the Manchu aristocracy consisted of 31 grades of nobility. The remainder of the Manchus were made bannermen in the Imperial Army, given land on which to settle, and exempted from Chinese local jurisdiction (Reischauer and Fairbank 1960). The Manchu language was kept alive by compulsory education, and Chinese classics were translated into Manchu. At the same time laws concerning the wearing of Manchu dress were enforced: Manchu people were not allowed to wear Chinese costume, while Chinese males were all compelled to wear the queue like their Manchu conquerors.

Under Manchu rule, the Qing dynasty was the period when China's boundaries reached their greatest extent. They stretched to Outer and Inner Mongolia in the north, to Tibet and Chinese Turkestan in the east, and to Taiwan to the west. The Manchu empire was divided into three parts: central, provincial and extra-provincial. The central government based in the capital in Beijing was headed by the emperor and the imperial family, and comprised the holders of high office. The second division comprised the eighteen provinces of China and the three provinces of Manchuria, while the extra-provincial divisions included the regions outside China proper known as Inner and Outer Mongolia, Xinjiang, and Tibet.

2
The Imperial Examinations

W HEN the new Manchu rulers took power in Beijing, their intention was to follow the system of government of the preceding Ming dynasty, but with checks on the weaknesses which had led to the downfall of previous dynasties. Gentry status, *shenshi*, was controlled by the government, and it was through this group that the government officials known as mandarins were selected. The word mandarin (*guan* in Chinese) is derived from the Portuguese word *mandar* which means to command. There were two orders of mandarins, the civil order who were responsible for the day-to-day affairs of the state, and the military order who were responsible for internal stablility and external defence.

The main route to becoming a mandarin and hence a member of the upper gentry, was by passing a series of qualifying examinations and becoming eligible for appointment to office. An alternative way was to purchase an academic degree and then an official rank and title. No proof of educational qualifications was required, although those who bought the title were usually literate. A man was then considered a member of the lower gentry. By allowing these two quasi groups and manipulating the rivalry between them was one way in which the Manchus attempted to keep the gentry in check (Chang 1970).

There were quotas for both Manchu and Chinese males, though from the very beginning the Manchu rulers admitted the Chinese into both civil and military office at all levels. The Chinese were not only better scholars than the Manchus, but there were many more Chinese conversant with an already established system.

These qualifying examinations had a long history in China. Some form of selection for office based on literary ability had been in use since the Tang dynasty (AD 618–906), although as far back as the Zhou period (1027–256 BC) there had been a primitive kind of selection based on talent. But it was during the Qing dynasty that the examination system reached its zenith, and, until its abolition in 1905, it was the surest means of social and material advancement.

The examinations were open to all males, with the exception of those classified as the 'mean people', in other words, the boat people, labourers, actors and musicians, executioners and torturers! The poorest man could become a distinguished official if he had the time and talent to pass these difficult examinations. Those with money and little ability, however, purchased degrees and official honours, while others obtained them through patronage and nepotism, or even bribery and cheating.

Normally, the number of degrees awarded was limited to the positions available in the government. There were men who spent their whole lives trying to pass the examinations. Unsuccessful candidates in their eighties and nineties were sometimes conferred with an honorary degree in acknowledgement of their life-long devotion to literary pursuits.

Education

Education and literacy were greatly prized. Writing equipment was revered and made from materials such as jade and other precious stones. The writing brush, paper, inkstone and ink were known as the 'four treasures' of the scholar's studio.

From a very early age, boys were groomed for success in the examinations. Even the games the children played related to their main objective: one such board game was called *shengguan tu* (the Game of Promotion). It was played on a board which represented the career of a mandarin from the lowest to the highest grade, according to the examination system. It was played with four dice, rather like Snakes and Ladders, and the object of each player was to secure promotion over the others.

Families often employed private tutors to educate their sons (girls were seldom even taught to read), or a private school for prospective candidates would be established by the clan or village in a study hall or within the ancestral hall. Successful candidates were highly regarded by successive generations of the clan, and tablets with the man's name and honour were hung in the ancestral hall.

At these schools boys from the age of seven were taught reading and writing by a teacher who was often himself a failed examination candidate. The school day lasted from sunrise to five in the afternoon with a break of only one hour. Teaching methods and materials had changed little over the past two thousand years. The boys studied the *Three Character Classic*, an essential school primer in which characters were arranged in columns of three, listing 'the elements, virtues, grains, domestic animals, social duties' and so on. These were memorized and recited to the teacher, which was known as 'backing the book' (see Fig. 2.1). As the boy grew older he would study the classic Chinese books such as the *Analects of Confucius*, the *Book of Changes*, and the *Book of Rites*, and even by the late nineteenth century could grow up learning nothing of arithmetic, geography, science or foreign languages.

Public colleges were founded by the district and provincial governments and were usually better organized than the clan schools

Fig. 2.1. 'Backing the Book', Students reciting from memory to the teacher, late nineteenth century. (*Source*: Smith 1894)

both in terms of curriculum and financial assistance for the students. One such college in Guangdong province, the Xuehai College, which was established by the governor of Guangdong and Guanxi in 1824 offered four courses. These were the study of history, the Confucian classics, literature, and philosophy.

Civil Examinations

At the age of about 18, a boy could be ready to take the *tongshi* or entrance examinations. The *junxiu* or 'man of promise' would take the first exam before the magistrate of the district where he lived, and a pass would entitle him to be called *tongsheng* or student.

The next hurdle was the annual examination for the first degree which was held in the prefectural city. A pass was compared by some to today's bachelor of arts degree and the student would become a *shengyuan*, or government student, colloquially known as *xiucai*, meaning 'budding talent'. Certain privileges accompanied a pass in this examination: the student became a member of the gentry class, and could erect a red sign over his door to indicate that he was a degree holder. He was exempt from corporal punishment, and was also entitled to government aid to enable him to continue his studies.

A graduating ceremony of the first degree was held at the literary chancellor's *yamen* (a walled establishment containing his residence and offices). The graduate wore a long blue silk gown and black satin boots. A red silk scarf was placed diagonally across the chest and tied under the opposite arm at the hip. On his head was a cone-shaped hat with two sprigs of artificial flowers made of gold leaf, or brass foil, fastened to wire. The tradition of the crossed red scarf and foil decorations is still seen today on some Cantonese bridegrooms in the New Territories of Hong Kong. Headmen in some villages there at important festivals such as the *Dajiao* (a ceremony held every ten years to pacify the dragon) also wear the decorations in their hats.

The second degree was held in the eighth moon of every third year in the provincial capitals, such as Guangzhou (Canton) in Guangdong. This was known as the degree *xiangshi* and was equivalent to a master of arts. A very small percentage of the candidates achieved success. Strict quotas, based in general on the size of the province, were imposed nationwide. Out of some 10,000 to 12,000 entrants, barely 300 would obtain their degree and be known as *juren* or 'promoted men' (Mayers 1896).

The provincial examination hall was a large area surrounded by high walls, with thousands of cells ranged along two sides of the compound. The candidates would spend several days confined to these poorly furnished, cramped and uncomfortable cells while they took the examination (see Figs. 2.2 and 2.3).

Fig. 2.2. Rows of cells in the Examination Hall; each row marked by a character from *The Thousand Character Classic*, Guangzhou, *c.* 1873. (*Source*: courtesy of Library of Congress, Washington, DC)

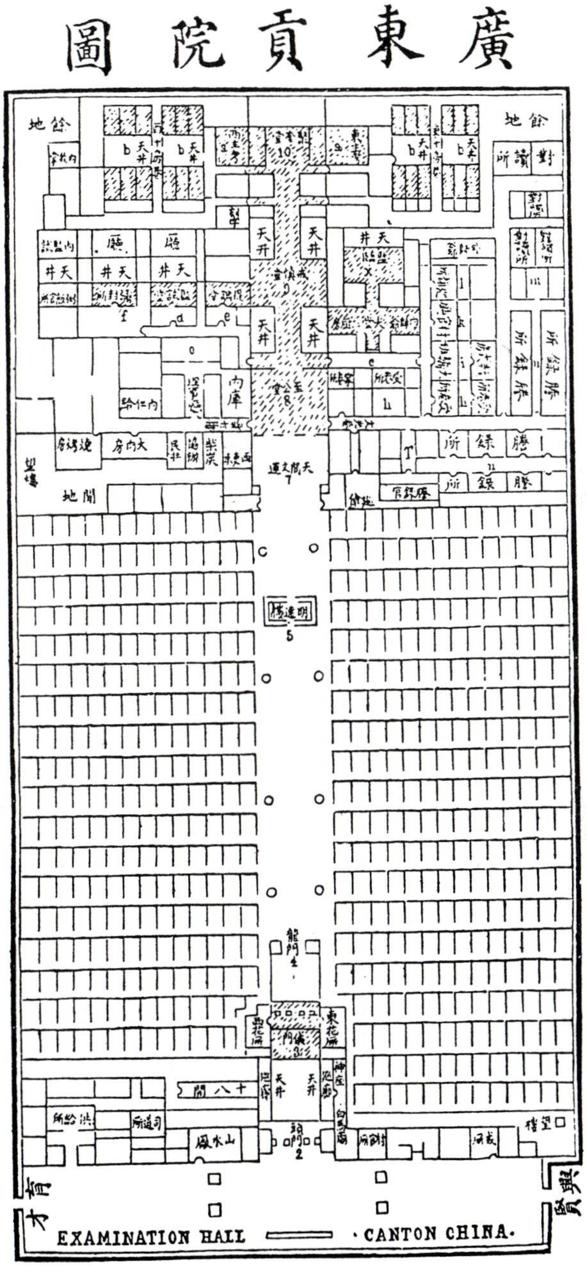

Fig 2.3. Native woodblock print showing one-sixteenth of the cells in the Examination Hall, Guangzhou. (*Source*: Thompson 1899)

The Canton Examination Halls cover sixteen acres of ground and are surrounded with a high wall. Access to the interior is only gained by two large and imposing gateways, duly guarded by watchmen. There are 8,653 cells in rows, running right and left of the central court and avenue, each cell being only five feet nine inches deep, three feet eight inches wide, ... Grooves are made in the walls of each cell, to admit a plank, which serves as table by day and bed by night. Once within, the candidates are not allowed to leave the enclosure during the examination, and the outer gates are sealed. In spite of all precautions, however, some are turned out each season for concealing 'cribs'. (Turner 1894)

The students were thoroughly searched on entry, however not only were crib sheets (see Fig. 2.4) smuggled in, but 'essay vendors are also at hand who receive notice of the text over the wall, and pass back the required essay by help of the watchman'! (Turner 1894)

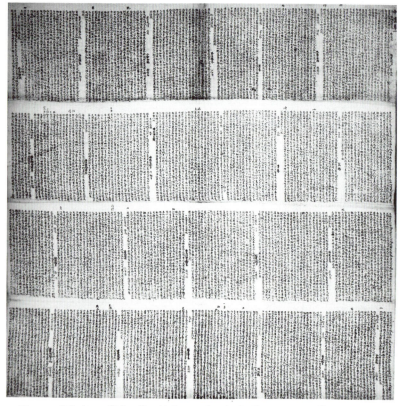

Fig. 2.4. Crib sheet: silk handkerchief covered on both sides in minute calligraphy in ink, of selections from the Classics; c. late Qing. (*Source*: reproduced by permission of the Oriental Ceramic Society of Hong Kong from *Art from the Scholar's Studio*, 1986)

The candidates had to remain in the enclosure for 36 hours, and took with them food and bedding. An official cook was attached to each row of cells. If a student died of fatigue and exposure, as happened now and again, his body would be passed over the wall and left there for his friends or family to remove. The examination comprised themes taken from the Chinese Classics, whereby the candidate had to write three essays and a poem. Calligraphy was always an important part of the examination, and the script had to be so carefully written that no correction or erasure was visible. Correct form was essential: each line had to have a certain number of words; the names of the emperor himself or his ancestors had to be at the start of a new line. Examiners were sent from Beijing to officiate.

At the second degree ceremony, graduates wore a flaring collar over the shoulders of the long gown, and the red scarf crossed the chest twice in the form of the letter 'X'. Then, in the spring of the year after they had passed the *xiangshi* examinations, the graduates were eligible to take a third degree, equivalent to a doctorate, for which they had to go to Beijing. Out of 6,000 graduates from all the provinces, only one fifth were expected to pass. This final metropolitan examination was known as *huishi* and those who graduated became *jinshi* ('finished scholars'). A final essay exam was taken within the precincts of the Imperial Palace and called the *dianshi*, or palace examination. According to their order of merit, one in three graduates would then be admitted into the prestigious Hanlin Academy. Success after the third degree level meant a high position in the government, especially if one graduated from this Academy.

Military Examinations

Not unnaturally, military examinations were based on physical feats, requiring little literary ability. A military degree was therefore never held in high esteem by the intellectual élite. It was not as important a requirement for military office, as was the civil degree for civil office (Smith 1974). Very often promotions and appointments were made on the basis of family connections or financial considerations. Those with some military education could purchase the *jiansheng* title as a short cut to military office, while the majority of officers in the Chinese Green Standard Army rose up through the ranks without obtaining a title or degree first.

Regular examinations were conducted by a department within the Board of War based in Beijing. The required essays were much shorter, with only a hundred or so characters to be written from memory from

Sunzi's famous treatise, the *Art of War*, or other classics to show the candidate's knowledge of military literature. The *wushengyuan*, or military government student, was examined by the same officials who invigilated at the literary examinations. The first degree exam also tested the candidate's ability in archery, both standing and on horseback, and in sword play. The emphasis on skill in archery continued throughout the nineteenth century when other nations had progressed to using modern firearms.

For the second degree, the candidate was examined by the provincial governor, and not by special commissioners from Beijing. The subject matter was similar in content to the first degree examination. The *wujuren* would then go to Beijing to take the third degree. Success meant immediate employment for the *wujinshi* in the army or navy anywhere in China.

3
The Role of the Mandarin

O N C E a man had successfully made his way through the examination system, his aim was to be appointed to a post as a government official. Graduates of the Hanlin Academy could expect to obtain posts within the Six Boards, which, along with the Imperial Chancery, were the two councils appointed to advise the emperor on the government of the country. Other graduates would receive appointments to provincial offices, depending on the level of their degree, and hoped, through further study or purchase, eventually to gain promotion to the higher ranks. By no means all those with degrees were able to find employment at the equivalent level and it sometimes took many years, after the man had lodged his application, for a post to become available.

Within the two orders, civil and military, there were nine ranks, each subdivided into principal and secondary classes, with a low supplementary rank for unclassed officials. Except at the highest level where civil and military were considered equal, civil officials were placed higher than military ones in the hierarchy: education and refinement, not courage, were considered the outstanding virtues. The Chinese place of honour on the left was reserved for civil mandarins while the military sat or walked on the right. Each mandarin was attached to a particular section of the administration, but during his career he could be employed to undertake judicial, administrative, and fiscal duties, being transferred from one post to another with little regard for his previous experience.

Hierarchy and Duties of the Provincial Mandarins

First ranking civil mandarins were employed in the central administration in the capital. In the provincial administration, the highest grade of second rank, principal class belonged to the viceroy or governor-general (*zongdu*, colloquial *zhitai*)(Marsh 1961). He could be in charge of one, often two, and sometimes three provinces. He had the rank of ex-officio President of the Board of War for, in addition to his civil duties, he would also be responsible for evaluating military officers, and regulating the Chinese Green Standard Army. The position of

LI HUNG-CHANG 李鸿章 *Anhui* M. 47 Fought against T'ai-p'ings 53. Taotai Fuhkien 59. Governor Kiangsu 62. Superintendent of Southern Trade Feb. 68. Governor-General Hukuang 67. Governor-General Chihli 70. Sen. Grand Secretary 75. Mourning 82. Acting Governor-General Chihli. Reappointed Governor-General and Grand Secretary Sept. 84. Has the title of *Po* or noble of 3rd order. Associate Director B³ of Admiralty Oct. 85. Granted Three-Eyed Peacock's Feather Feb. 94. Deprived of Peacock's Feather and Yellow Riding Jacket Sept. 94. Deprived of rank but retained at post Dec. 94. Envoy to Japan to sue for peace 95. Transferred to Peking Aug. 95. Mission to Coronation of Tsar Nicholas II 96. Tsung-li Yamên Oct. 96. Relieved of duty at the Tsung-li Yamên Sept. 98. Ordered to inspect Yellow River Nov. 98. Imperial Commissioner for Trade Nov. 99. Acting Governor General Liang Kuang Dec. 99. Governor General Dᵒ May 00. Governor General Chihli June 00. Appointed Peace Plenipotentiary Aug. 00. Council of Government Reform April 01. Died Nov. 01. Granted posthumous rank as Marquis and name of Wen-chung (" Learned and Loyal ").

LI KUANG-CHIU 李光久 *Hunan* P.G. Son of Li Hsü-pin, former Governor of Anhui. Has title of nobility of 5th order. Acting Taotai for some time at Wênchow. Kung-Ch'in-Chieh Tao Kansu Oct. 95. Au-Lu-Ch'u-Ho Tao Anhui Aug. 96. Vacated post (illness) Sept. 96. Fêng-Ying-Liu-Ssŭ Tao Anhui May 97. Su-Sung-T'ai Tao (Shanghai) Nov. 98. Jud. Comm. Chekiang May 99. Died Jan. 00.

LI LIEN-FANG 李聯芳 *Shensi* M. 71. Expositor Hanlin Aut. 01. Assistant Supervisor of Instruction.

LI MIN-SHÊN 李岷琛 *Szechuan.* M. 71. Tso-chiang Tao Kuangsi Mar. 91. Mourning May 93. Taotai Tientsin Aug. 95. Customs Taotai Tientsin Dec. 96. Grain Intendant Kiangsi Dec. 98. Jud. Comm. Hupeh Feb. 01.

LI NAN-HUA 李南華 Brigadier General at Ting-chou (Fukien).

LI P'EI-JUNG 李培榮 *Yünnan* M.S. Commander-in-Chief Kansu. Cashiered Jan. 95.

LI PING-HÊNG 李秉衡 *Fêng-t'ien* P. Fin. Comm. Kuangsi July 85. Retired Oct. 87. Governor Anhui May 94. Governor Shantung Aug. 94. Appointed Viceroy of Szechuan Sept. 97, but did not proceed. Vacated post Dec. 97. Degraded two steps and transferred Feb. 98. Special Mission to Moukden Sept. 99. Special Commissioner to Yangtse Provinces Dec. 99. Assistant Generalissimo of Northern Forces July 00. Committed suicide Nov. 00. Sentence of death recorded Feb. 01.

Fig. 3.1. A page of information and dates of mandarins' graduation, promotion, and so forth. (Abbreviations are as follows: M. 47: Metropolitan Graduate of the year 1847; P.G: Provincial Graduate: M.S.: Military Service; P.: Purchase.) (*Source:* Ker 1903)

12

viceroy was considered to be one of the most important in the land as it involved direct communication with the emperor, whose will the viceroy would pass down to subordinate mandarins.

Below the viceroy was the governor (*xunfu*, colloquial *futai*), a second rank, secondary class mandarin with similar power to that of the viceroy, but who was in charge of the civil and military affairs of a single province. The viceroy considered him a colleague rather than a subordinate. Next came the financial controller (*buzheng shisi*, colloquial *fantai*) who was the head of the civil service in each province and treasurer of the provincial exchequer. In times of war or unrest he was responsible for the funding of military supplies. The provincial judge (*ancha shisi*, colloquial *nietai*) had the highest judicial authority in the province, in real terms above that of the viceroy. He was followed by the salt and grain commissioners, marine inspectors, and other senior officials.

A province was divided into a number of prefectures, then subdivided into departments and districts. Each district was administered by a magistrate and several assistant magistrates. These lower-ranking mandarins had many duties and were, at the same time, judge, tax collector, director of police, and sheriff of the district. They also assumed some military duties and, in an emergency, sometimes took an active part in military affairs.

Although the viceroy and governor had general administrative control of the military forces in their province, they did not control the banner garrisons in which were stationed the famous Eight Banners. This had been originally an exclusively Manchu army, instrumental in the overthrow of the Ming empire. But from the start of the Qing period, it consisted of 24 banners or units, made up of eight banners of Manchu soldiers, and eight of Chinese soldiers plus eight of Mongolian soldiers who were direct descendants of those who had assisted in the conquest of China. Even so, throughout the Qing dynasty Manchu soldiers outnumbered Chinese and Mongols by about three to one (Smith 1974). These banner garrisons, of which more than half were situated in Beijing, and the rest in China's major cities, were commanded by Manchu generals.

The second of the two regular armies within the Qing administration was entirely Chinese, known as the Green Standard Army. Responsible for the defence and internal security of the country, it also had many official duties to provide guards, prevent crime, provide escort services, and so on, as it was more of a constabulary than an army. Soldiers of the Green Standard Army joined for life and had hereditary tenure. One feature of the check system operated by the Qing rulers, was that Manchu generals shared the responsibility for the

Green Standard Army with a provincial commander-in-chief known as a *tidu* who was under the indirect control of the civil official.

Beneath the *tidu* was the brigade-general (*zongbing*) who, generally speaking, commanded a brigade. Next in line came the colonel (*fujiang*), the lieutenant-colonel (*canjiang*), the major (*youji*), first captain (*dusi*), and the second captain (*shoubei*), each of whom commanded a battalion. These battalions were further divided into military posts each commanded by a lieutenant (*qianzong*), a sergeant (*bazong*), a second sergeant (*waiwei qianzong*), or a corporal (*waiwei bazong*) (Smith 1974).

A military *yamen* was situated in Tai O, on Lantau Island in Hong Kong, which was Chinese territory until the British takeover in 1898. A local historian, Dr James Hayes, recalls being told by a Hong Kong business man, who spent his schooldays on the island in the 1890s, of the *yamen* with its large table in the main room, with flags and banners placed upon it. A senior officer, who was a second sergeant, sat behind it, wearing a long gown on the front of which was an embroidered badge decorated with an animal.

Promotion within the military ranks of the Green Standard Army was usually based on performance, obtaining a degree in the military examinations or hereditary rank. Viceroys and governors nominated candidates for posts ranging from colonel to second captain, while at the lowest level men were raised through the ranks, or taken from the local population.

Salary

The salary of a mandarin was not high. He was paid six months in advance; he was also paid expenses on government business, was exempt from taxes and allowed to borrow from public stock sums in proportion to his rank. This low salary however resulted in a tendency to corruption.

A Viceroy in the provinces gets as his yearly official salary about £100, and allowances amounting to £900 or £1,200 more; but he has to defray out of these sums all his yamen expenses, including stationery, etc., salaries, and food to his secretaries, writers, and A.D.C., his body-guards and general retinue, to entertain his innumerable guests, and send his annual tributes to the various high officials in the capital, to say nothing of supporting his high station and his numerous family … to meet his expenditure he would require no less than £10,000 or £15,000 per annum … From these high magnates downwards, the Chinese officials are underpaid in the same proportion, until we get to the lowest grade, the petty mandarin, whose official pay is scarcely better than that

of a well-paid Hongkong coolie, and the soldiers and sailors who receive four
to ten shillings a month, subject oftentimes to various unjust deductions and
squeezes by their superiors. (Dyer Ball 1925)

Life could be arduous for a mandarin, both physically and
financially. However there were some areas of China, especially some
rich districts of Guangdong province, where the phrase '*shui shui, tso
shui, tsou shui*' (literally 'sleeping income, sitting income, walking
income') applied. In other words, whether an official slept, sat, or
simply strolled around, his emoluments kept coming in regardless
(Morse 1908).

Regulations of Behaviour

Civil mandarins were expected to resign from office on the death of a
parent. The period of mourning was three years (in actual fact, 27
months) for which he had to return to his ancestral home. Not to do so
was considered an offence in Chinese law. Military mandarins of the
first three ranks did likewise, but lower-ranking military mandarins
were permitted to be absent for shorter periods. The expense and
inconvenience to the mandarin could be great, especially if he worked
in southern China and his ancestral home was in a northern province.
Since officials were not allowed to serve in their own districts this was
quite likely to be the case.

Mandarins were subject to regulations aimed at ordering their
behaviour in public. For example, they were not allowed to go about
on foot, but had to travel in a sedan chair accompanied by the proper
number of attendants; attending theatrical events was forbidden except
during certain festivals, and so was gambling. However, it seems that
both in public and in private, a mandarin was a law unto himself as far
as these restrictions were concerned, with the exception of walking!
(See Fig. 3.3.)

If a mandarin failed in his duty or violated the law (and did not
succeed in concealing it), he might offer large bribes to the higher officials to prevent them from reporting him to the court in Beijing. If the
culprit was a high official, such as a viceroy, whom the emperor wished
to punish by execution, the latter would indicate his displeasure by
sending the guilty mandarin a silken cord. This was an invitation to the
mandarin to strangle himself. The Imperial Commissioner Ge Ying
failed in the negotiations between the Beijing government and the
British government led by Lord Elgin which resulted in the Treaty of
Tianjin and the subsequent opening up of the new treaty ports. He was
recalled to Beijing and 'on his arrival, the silken cord was sent to him,

Official Title in Chinese	Official Title in English	Title used in direct Address. In Chinese (used after the surname or alone.)	Title used in direct Address. (Equivalent) in English.	Class	Button	Salary (varying with the Rank) £	Abr[...]estation (alternates varying with each Post.) £
tsüng tuh or chi tai	Governor-General	大人 ta jin	Your Excellency	1	Plain & Red	60	8333
hsün fu or fu tai	Governor	ditto	ditto	2	Flowered & Red	50	4333
pu ching si	Superintendent of Finances	ditto	ditto	2	ditto	ditto	2666
ancha si	Governal Judge	ditto	ditto	3	Transparent Blue	43	2000
yen yun si	Collector of the Salt Gabel	ditto	ditto	3	ditto	ditto	1666
leang chu tau	Grain Collector	ditto	ditto	4	Opaque Blue	35	1266
shün hsün tau	Intendant of Circuit	大夫爺 ta lau ye	Your Honor	4	ditto	ditto	1000 †
chi fu	Prefect of Department	ditto	ditto	4	ditto	ditto	652
chi li chi chou	Prefect of Inferior Department	ditto	ditto	5	Uncolored Glass	26	383
chi li ting chi	Independent Sub-Prefect	ditto	ditto	5	ditto	ditto	300
tüng chi	Sub-Prefect	ditto	ditto	5	ditto	ditto	225
tüng pan	Deputy Sub-Prefect	ditto	ditto	6	White	20	176
chi chou	District Magistrate	ditto	ditto	5	Uncolored Glass	26	262
chi hsien	ditto	大爺 tai ye	Your Worship	7	Plain Gilt	15	262
hsien ching or tso tang	Assistant District-Magistrate	ditto	ditto	8	Gilt with Flowers in relief	13	All titles, from
chu pu	Township Magistrate	ditto	ditto	9	Gilt with engraved Flowers	11	the District Magis-
hsün chien	Inspector of Police	ditto	ditto	9	ditto	ditto	trate downwards,
li mu	ditto	ditto	ditto	9	ditto	ditto	goes about £22,
tien shi	ditto	ditto	ditto	undassed	ditto	ditto	with the exception
gho pô su	Inspector of River Police	ditto	ditto	undassed	ditto	ditto	of the Treasurer

16

Fig. 3.2. A page showing the 'Titles, Rank, and Legal Income of the Mandarins'. (*Source:* Meadows 1847). Note: some authorities grade the Governor-General as second rank (see page 11).

Fig. 3.3. A mandarin in a sedan chair on a ceremonial visit, drawn by Thomas Allom. (*Source*: Wright 1843)

the significance of which he understood, and he ended his life by strangulation' (Hunter 1911). If a man delayed committing suicide, he was beheaded, a less honourable death than the former. Strangulation was preferred as it left the body intact which was important for the afterlife.

A mandarin's love of pomp and ceremony was nowhere more apparent than when he appeared in public *en route* to meet a visitor or to take part in a festival. The procession of a low-ranking mandarin carrying out his everyday affairs was often only slightly less in size and stature than a viceroy's procession which contained:

Two men bearing gongs and flags in front.

Ten or more men or boys carrying red oblong boards, with handles attached, having various inscriptions; some of these denote the officer's rank, command people to keep silence, and order idlers to get out of the way.

Two men on horseback.

Two men, one carrying a large official fan and the other a large umbrella of state.

Two men carrying a trunk full of changes of clothing.

Eight men carrying whips, whose business it is to clear the way, call out when passing the yamuns of other officials, and when turning round corners.

Four men carrying censers having burning incense.

Four men carrying swords.

Two men, whose business in part is to receive petitions, if presented in the street.

Four men to steady the sedan of the mandarin.

Four men on horseback, holding each a flag having a long handle.

Sixteen soldiers following the sedan, carrying swords, spears, flags, hammers, iron chains, etc.

On occasions when he wishes to appear with more extraordinary pomp and parade, he employs more men and more soldiers. When he pleases, he may dispense with many of the usual attendants. (Doolittle 1895)

Everything relating to the mandarin's procession was conducted strictly according to the rules. Each official had a certain number of bearers according to his rank. Cannons were fired when the highest ranks left their *yamen*, when they entered the *yamen* of another official, and again when they returned home. In the procession would be flag bearers who would beat the gong at regular intervals. When a high official appeared in the street it was obligatory for all passers-by to stop, for sedan chairs to be put down, and people on horseback to dismount. Anyone who did not comply was liable to be beaten unmercifully. These regulations, however, only applied to mandarins of above fourth rank, below that life carried on as usual.

Fig. 3.4. A mandarin's travelling boat. He is attended by servants, while his wife sits under a canopy at the stern. The double umbrella and flag indicate the importance of the occupant. (*Source:* Alexander 1805)

4
The Dress of the Mandarin

IN order to establish full control over the Han Chinese people, the Manchu emperors decreed that their customs, language, and particularly their style of clothing, should be adopted by the conquered race. By 1759, the Qianlong emperor was sufficiently concerned that the Manchu costume was being diluted by the Chinese style that he compiled an edict entitled *The Illustrated Catalogue of Ritual Paraphernalia of the Qing Dynasty* (*Huangchao liqi tushi*), which was published and enforced in 1766. This contained a series of regulations governing the style of dress to be worn on all official occasions for everyone employed in the service of the Manchu government, up to and including the emperor himself.

Additionally, there were rules governing the changing of clothing from season to season, the timing of which was ordered by an edict issued in the *Official Gazette* from Beijing. This stated the month, day, and hour that the emperor would change from winter clothing to summer clothing and so on. At this time all those wearing official dress were obliged to do likewise.

Official Clothing

Clothing was classified as official and non-official attire and further subdivided into formal, semi-formal, and informal. Mandarins, both Manchu and Han Chinese, wore Manchu-style robes for formal occasions such as government business, celebrations and festivals, but the Chinese were allowed to wear their own Han Chinese-style robes for informal occasions (Vollmer 1983).

The Manchus, having been hunters, had developed their style of clothing from the skins of the animals they caught. Official formal clothing consisted of the *chaofu* or court robe which preserved some of the features of original Manchu costume from pre-conquest times, and was worn by the emperor down to the higher-ranking mandarins at court for all important ritual occasions, such as the annual state sacrifice.

Thought originally to have been made of two parts (although some historians contend that it was always the one-piece outfit it later became), the *chaofu* consisted of a short side-fastening riding jacket, worn with paired aprons to give the necessary impression of bulk traditionally associated with festival garments. The curved overlapping right front was a shape derived from an animal skin, and fastened with loops and toggles, again nomadic in origin. The long fitted sleeves had horizontal ribbing of a different fabric, thought to have developed so that the wearer could bend his arm more easily when hunting. The sleeves ended in horse-hoof cuffs, originally intended to protect the hands when the wearer was riding in bad weather, and during the Qing to cover the hands, especially on formal occasions when it was considered impolite to show them. By the end of the eighteenth century the top and skirt were joined together as one with a small flap called a *ren* at the side to cover the fastening.

The court robes, which during the Qing dynasty were made of silk, were richly embroidered with dragons on chest, back, and shoulders, with a band of dragons on the skirt, in varying arrangements according to the status of the owner and style of the time (see Fig. 4.1) (Cammann 1944−5).

Fig. 4.1. *Chaofu*, official formal court dress, 1875−1900. (*Source*: Teresa Coleman Fine Arts, Hong Kong)

The colours of the robes were carefully regulated and certain colours were reserved for the emperor and his immediate family. Blue was the dynastic colour and replaced red which had been the Ming dynasty colour. It was worn by the lower-ranking princes, mandarins, and the peasants who wore indigo dyed cotton. In the imperial family, bright yellow was reserved for the emperor, although he could wear other colours if he wished or if the occasion demanded it; orange or 'apricot yellow' was for the heir apparent; brown, called 'tawny yellow' was for the imperial princes. Third and fourth degree princes and noblemen wore blue, unless they had been given the honour of wearing 'tawny yellow' by the emperor. Civil and military mandarins wore blue-black.

Around the neck was worn the flared collar known as *piling* or shoulder collar. This was asymmetrical in shape, said to have developed from a hood which had been opened out along the top of the crown to extend beyond the shoulders. It was usually embroidered or woven with dragon designs with a border around the edge, and was attached to the top button of the *chaofu* or fastened independently.

Fig. 4.2. Liu Changyu, governor-general of Guangdong and Guangxi wearing official formal court attire of *pufu* with civil rank badge, and *chaofu*, with *piling*, 1863. (*Source*: photo by M. Miller, Royal Asiatic Society of Great Britain and Northern Ireland)

For less important court occasions and official or government business, semi-formal official clothing colloquially known as 'full dress' was worn. This comprised a long robe called a *qifu*, with the *piling* and a surcoat bearing the badges of rank (see Fig.4.3).

Fig. 4.3. Portrait of a mandarin wearing official semi-formal attire (also known as 'full dress'), with *pufu*, *qifu*, *piling*, with winter hat and peacock plume with two 'eyes', late eighteenth century. (*Source*: Mason 1804)

The *qifu*, otherwise known among Westerners as a dragon robe, was a full-length coat with sleeves and a curved overlapping right front based originally, like the top half of the *chaofu*, on animal skins, with two at the front and one at the back. To make it easier to ride in, the Manchus later added slits at the front and back hem in addition to those at the sides. It was richly embroidered with dragons and propitious symbols:

The *ch'i–fu* [*qifu*] is a schematic diagram of the universe ... . The lower border of diagonal bands and rounded billows represents water; at the four axes of the coat, the cardinal points, rise prism-shaped rocks symbolizing the earth mountain. Above is the cloud-filled firmament against which dragons, the symbols of imperial authority, coil and twist. The symbolism is complete only when the coat is worn. The human body becomes the world axis; the neck opening, the gate of heaven or apex of the universe, separates the material world of the coat from the realm of the spiritual represented by the wearer's head. (Vollmer 1977) (See Fig. 4.4.)

Fig. 4.4. *Qifu*, official semi-formal dress; also worn for non–official formal occasions, late nineteenth century. (*Source*: author's collection)

In the early part of the dynasty, the mountains and clouds were towering and bold, but later became shorter and unnatural, while the *lishui* or diagonal lines became much longer.

Colours for the *qifu* were in accordance with those for the *chaofu* for all ranks from the emperor down to the lowest-ranking mandarin.

First, second and third rank mandarins could wear nine four-clawed dragons (*mangpao*) embroidered on the robe. Dragons were placed one each at the front and back of the chest, one at each shoulder, and two at the front and back hem. The symbolic ninth dragon was hidden inside the front inside flap of the robe, the number nine being associated with man in ancient Taoist numerology. Fourth to sixth rank civil and military officials wore eight four-clawed dragons. The five-clawed dragons (*longpao*), normally a symbol of the emperor, were also worn by lower ranks if they had been awarded the privilege. Towards the end of the dynasty, most mandarins wore them whether permitted to or not (Cammann 1952).

Officials of the seventh to ninth rank, and unclassified officials were supposed to wear five four-clawed dragons, but this regulation does not seem to have been enforced, and low-ranking officials would seldom have needed to wear dragon robes. Those with a low income would not have been able to afford one, and the wealthy would have obtained a higher-ranking robe by influence or purchase. At the end of the dynasty when traditions were breaking down, the lowest officials could have worn an eight dragon robe if the occasion warranted it.

A calf-length centre-fastening surcoat was introduced after 1759, and all who appeared at court were required to wear it, regardless of background or income. Usually called a *pufu* (meaning 'garment with a patch'), but sometimes *waidao* (meaning 'outer covering'), it was made from blue-black or purple-black satin. For winter it was often lined or edged with white fur (sable fur was reserved for mandarins of third rank and above), for spring and autumn the lining was cotton, and the garment itself was made of silk gauze and unlined for the summer. A roundel design was frequently incorporated into the weave.

The *pufu* was a loose-fitting coat made of two lengths of cloth, folded at the shoulders and opening down the centre front, with side and back vents. The short sleeves and the fact that the coat reached mid-calf enabled the wearer to show off the sleeves and embroidered hem of the *chaofu* or *qifu* underneath. In addition, the simple shape of the coat made it an ideal background for the badges of rank fixed to front and back. Prior to the introduction of the *pufu*, badges of rank were applied directly to the *chaofu*.

Official informal clothing was worn for other events which were not connected with major ceremonies or governing. It was considered bad taste to wear formal robes on private occasions, at home or when visiting friends. A *changfu* or plain long gown of silk, usually reddish-brown, grey, or blue, and cut in the same style as the *qifu*, was worn under the *pufu*. Low-ranking officials would generally also wear the *changfu* under a *pufu* on semi-formal occasions.

24

During the second half of the nineteenth century, it became the fashion to wear a small plain stiffened collar (*lingtou*) which fitted over the *pufu*. This was made of silk, velvet, or fur according to the season, and worn sometimes with the *piling*, or by itself on informal occasions (see Fig. 4.5).

Fig. 4.5. Studio photo of a mandarin of the fourth rank in official informal dress of *pufu* and *lingtou*, and showing cuffs of *changfu* turned back, *c.* 1900. (*Source*: author's collection)

Non-official Clothing

The second group of regulations for non-official occasions was also subdivided into three categories. In practice, however, the non-official formal clothing which was worn when the mandarin was in the public view for celebrations, festivals, birthdays and family gatherings was the same as the official semi-formal clothing, except that the *lingtou* was worn over the *qifu* and *pufu*, in place of the *piling*.

Non-official semi-formal wear and informal wear was called 'half dress' which indicated that the mandarin did not need to wear his badge of rank. Semi-formal attire consisted of the *changfu* worn with the *pufu* and *lingtou* (see Fig 4.6). For informal wear at home and out of the public eye the *changfu* was worn on its own, sometimes combined with a short, sleeveless waistcoat, or more often with a *magua*.

Fig. 4.6. Two mandarins of the sixth rank wearing winter (on left) and summer non-official semi-formal attire, also known as 'half dress', mid-nineteenth century. (*Source*: Meadows 1847)

The *magua* or, literally, riding jacket replaced the *pufu* as formal dress at the end of the dynasty. It was a short jacket cut like the *pufu* but reaching only to the hips (see Fig. 4.7). It fastened down the centre front with loops and buttons and later had a small stand-up collar. There were short slits at side-seams and centre back, and it was made of black silk damask, often with roundels woven into the design. Before pockets were introduced into the side seams or on to the inside flap of the gown at the end of the last century, the jacket's or gown's wide sleeves doubled as a place to keep small objects. A 'sleeve full of snuff', 'sleeve editions' (small books), and even 'sleeve dogs' (small Pekinese or lap dogs) were all carried there.

Fig. 4.7. Mandarins at the opening of the Kowloon–Canton Railway in Hong Kong, wearing *magua* and *changfu*, 1911. (*Source*: Hong Kong Museum of History, Urban Council, Hong Kong)

Accessories

A more usual way of carrying small objects was from a girdle which tightly belted the gown. Attached to the girdle hung all the essentials of daily life: the fan case, snuff bottle, tobacco pouch, a pair of chopsticks in a case with a knife, an archer's ring, and later, a most valued possession, a watch. Girdle clasps made with precious or semi-precious stones denoted rank, and were the same for civil and military alike.

Rank	Girdle clasp
First	jade set with rubies
Second	gold set with rubies
Third	worked gold
Fourth	worked gold with silver button
Fifth	worked gold with plain silver button
Sixth	mother-of-pearl
Seventh	silver
Eighth	clear horn
Ninth	buffalo horn

A mandarin was seldom seen without his hat, and then only in the private quarters of his home. Hats were worn irrespective of the degree of formality and officialdom, and were changed according to season. In winter, from the eighth month in the Chinese calendar, the hat had a turned-up brim of black satin, fur, or velvet, with the crown covered in red fringing. Some hats had a false queue of silk or hair attached to supplement the wearer's own lack of hair.

In summer, from the third month of the Chinese calendar, the hat was a conical shape, made of woven straw for the lower ranks, and split bamboo for the higher officials. When first introduced in 1646 'there were none in the shops in south China, and they had to be cut out of baskets and mats' (Wilson 1986). Towards the end of the dynasty, Shandong province was supplying nearly the whole of China with straw summer hats, while a cottage industry in villages around Chengdu in Sichuan province supplied those made of finely woven bamboo netting covered with silk gauze. These took two days or more to weave (Wilson 1986). Inside the conical hats was a stiff circle of woven rattan covered in red cotton with strings to tie under the chin. Fringes of red silk cords or dyed horse-hair or goat-hair covered the crown from apex to edge.

Distinctions were made between civil and military mandarins with the use of bird for the former, and animal for the latter on the badges of rank, but as with the girdle clasp, both types of mandarin wore the same kind of cap button on the hat. These finials, or buttons as they were called by foreigners, were worn at the apex of the hat and meant that the mandarin's rank could be identified at a glance. They were more conspicuous than rank badges, especially as the badges were only worn on 'full dress' occasions. At first the buttons were of precious stones or gold, but later in the dynasty they were apparently made of glass or brass.

Rank	Cap finial
First	transparent ruby
Second	opaque coral
Third	transparent sapphire
Fourth	opaque lapis lazuli
Fifth	transparent crystal
Sixth	opaque jade
Seventh	plain gold
Eighth	worked gold with *shou* character
Ninth	worked gold with two *shou* characters

For the fifth rank and above, peacock feathers (*huayu*) would be attached to the cap button through a jade tube. These were worn on public occasions and seen as a sign of great honour accorded by the emperor for services rendered, or in the case of soldiers, for bravery. One, two or three peacock feathers were worn: the more eyes, the greater the honour. However, towards the end of the dynasty, these were openly for sale. One example in the Victoria and Albert Museum in London still bears the label from the Wan Sheng Yong Feather Shop in the main street in Beijing. Officials and officers of the sixth rank and below used blue quills (*lanyu*) from the raven's tail.

A necklace of 108 beads of coral, jade or other precious and semi-precious stones would be worn by both the mandarin and his wife. Sometimes referred to as a mandarin chain, it had developed from a Buddhist rosary sent in 1643 by the Dalai Lama to the Manchu ruler. Three counting strings were also added by the Manchus, and were worn with two strings on the left for men, and two strings on the right for the mandarin's wife. Four large beads of contrasting stone known as *fotou* were said to represent the four seasons and were placed between groups of 27 beads. On the *fotou* bead between the counting strings was a long drop extension called a *beiyun* (back cloud) which hung down the back and served both as a counterweight and an ornament. Civil officials of the fifth rank and above, and military officials of fourth rank and above, were required to wear the chain.

Black satin boots, an indication that the wearer never left home except in a sedan chair, were an important but expensive part of the mandarin's regalia and said to cost as much as a servant's wage for one year (Wilson 1986). They were made with the leg part longer than was necessary so that the satin lay in folds around the ankle. The soles were up to seven centimetres thick and were made of layers of felted paper, whitened round the edges, and were shorter than the uppers at the toe to make it easier for the wearer to walk.

The Mandarin's Wife

Women were excluded from government and made few public appearances. However, within the family, senior women had status and were well respected, being accorded a position of honour at important domestic events and festivals.

Manchu mandarins' wives were bound by the same regulations for official and non-official attire as their husbands, with subdivisions for degrees of formality. For semi-formal and informal occasions, a wife wore a long gown, side-fastening with long wide sleeves ending in horsehoof cuffs. Over it was worn the *pufu* or an embroidered sleeveless vest bearing the same badge of rank as her husband, or father if she was single. For informal wear she wore a short centre-opening jacket, or side-fastening sleeveless vest.

The headdress worn by a Manchu woman was very elaborate. It was made of black satin with bat-wing shapes characteristic of nomadic headwear from the Eurasian steppe. Originally the hair itself was set and shaped in this way, but during the nineteenth century, the hair was replaced by black satin as being more practical and easier to keep in order. It was decorated with several artificial flowers and hair ornaments. Manchu women did not bind their feet, and wore boat-shaped shoes with a high centre heel, either concave or convex in shape (see Fig. 4.8).

Fig. 4.8. Manchu woman with typical Manchu headdress in non-official informal dress of long robe and sleeveless vest, end nineteenth century. (*Source*: Putnam Weale 1904)

As someone of little consequence in the Manchu government, the Chinese mandarin's wife wore no official attire. On non-official formal occasions when she appeared with her husband she wore a different style of dress from her Manchu counterpart. This comprised a voluminous side-fastening gown with wide sleeves, richly embroidered like that of the Manchu woman's but reaching to just below the knee. Over this was worn a sleeveless vest with a fringe at the hem, which bore the same badge of rank as her husband or, if she were unmarried, her father (see Fig. 4.9). A four-pointed collar was worn either as a separate accessory or incorporated into the jacket, with the four lobes hanging at the chest, back and over each shoulder. For less formal occasions, the vest was replaced by the *pufu* or short, side-fastening sleeveless jacket.

A skirt was worn with the jacket. It was made of paired aprons

Fig. 4.9. Possibly the wife of Huang Cantang, governor of Guangdong, wearing Chinese non-official formal dress and insignia square denoting second civil rank, *c.* 1862. (*Source*: Hardy 1905)

attached to a waistband rather like the Manchu *chaofu*, but with two embroidered panels at back and front and pleats to each side of the panels. Loose trousers were worn under the skirt. The Chinese woman did not adopt the fanciful Manchu headdress. On important occasions a lattice base, to which were attached many kingfisher feathers and jewelled hairpins, imitated an upswept hairstyle and was placed on top of the wearer's hair.

Chinese women, from all but the lowest level of society and some ethnic minority groups in the south such as the Hakka women in Guangdong and Fujian, bound their feet from early childhood and wore tiny embroidered silk shoes, sometimes only eight centimetres long. This had been the custom for over a thousand years; the Manchus on taking power had tried to ban it, but were unsuccessful and it lasted until it was outlawed by the new Republic in 1912, finally dying out in the 1930s.

5

The Development of Mandarin Squares

B e f o r e insignia badges, and indeed cap finials, were introduced to denote a person's rank, ornamental hoop belts inlaid with precious stones were the only regulated identification imposed at the beginning of the Ming dynasty. Persian miniatures and Chinese wood-block prints depict Mongol nobles wearing ornamental square plaques with floral or bird and animal scenes woven directly on to the fabric of their robes at chest and back during the preceding Yuan dynasty (Cammann 1944–5). These plaques did not denote rank, and were most probably only decorative, but the Ming court must have been influenced by them when they decided, twenty years after seizing power and wiping out the last of the Mongol resistance, to introduce badges of rank.

Ming Badges

Insignia badges made their appearance in 1391, following exact regulations for clothing for all occasions, and were the only major innovation to costume introduced by the very conservative Ming dynasty. The emperor's yellow robe was based on the side-fastening style of the Song dynasty (960–1279), and he and his sons wore circular badges with coiled dragons, woven or embroidered in gold, and placed at chest, back, and one at each shoulder. Noblemen and scholars wore amply cut robes of red silk (the dynastic colour) with a woven square at front and back called *puzi* depicting a man's rank.

Ming festival squares and roundels were common towards the end of the dynasty, especially by the time of the Wanli reign (1572–1620). These badges, which were worn by members of the imperial household, appeared on several occasions throughout the year: the emperor's birthday, Lunar New Year, the Dragon Boat Festival and many others. Reasons given for the abundance of festivals throughout the year include the suggestion that the Mongol rulers of the preceding Yuan dynasty had suppressed Chinese festivals so that none was celebrated officially. Secondly, continued pressure from Mongol and Manchu forces in the north during the latter part of the dynasty meant that celebrations were seen as relaxing diversions for the beleaguered Ming officials. Finally, the court eunuchs who had great control over the imperial family enjoyed the relief from monotony and hoped that with constant preparation for festivals, the court would have little time to try and change the status quo (Cammann 1953).

Symbols on the badges were to evoke good fortune and long life, especially the *shou* character and the Eight Precious Things. Often two symbols were combined to make the square suitable for two occasions, for example a gourd on a New Year badge would have a canopy resembling a lantern placed over it, thus making it appropriate for the Lantern Festival held two weeks later.

Ming squares had no real border, and were very broad, but the top edge of the square was often from three to six centimetres narrower than the bottom edge, presumably so that the sides of the square would not be hidden by the wearer's arms. Insignia for male members of the imperial family depicted the *qilin* or *baize*, with the dragon reserved for the emperor and his sons. Insignia for the female members depicted a phoenix. These squares were woven or embroidered directly on to the fabric before the robe was assembled, so the square was bisected by a centre seam.

Officials and noblemen wore a square sewn to the robe, which could be replaced if the wearer's rank changed. Civil officials were depicted by birds and military officials by animals. The right to wear these insignia was bestowed by the emperor, and the official then had it made for himself. At first, some ranks had a choice of two birds or animals. This was because the square, made of gold thread, was very costly, and so an official who was temporarily promoted, or who was expecting promotion, could either wear the higher-ranking square or continue to wear the lower-ranking one. However, the gain in 'face' was considered worth the extra expense and the higher rank was almost always worn. It was found that certain ambitious officials were taking advantage of being allowed a choice, and in 1527 all officials were ordered to wear insignia only of their own rank. At the same time, only one bird depicted each rank, though regulations for military ranks remained unchanged (Cammann 1944–5).

At first, in the early Ming squares, two birds were shown in a balanced composition, poised in flight, but later in the dynasty this was replaced by one bird perched on a rock or branch with the other flying down from above. Flowering plants filled out the square and towards the end of the dynasty many symbols were added to bring luck to the wearer. Once the idea of the two balanced birds was changed in late Ming, single birds began to appear and a highly stylized bird developed.

Most of the Ming squares that have survived are of *kesi* (see Chapter 9), though possibly more delicately embroidered ones were made that have not survived. The areas manufacturing woven silk products suffered during the Manchu invasion, and the resulting high costs, coupled with the fact that woven silk may have been an imperial monopoly, meant that almost all early Qing squares were embroidered. *Kesi* ones did not reappear in any quantity until the mid-nineteenth century.

Qing Badges

On taking power in 1644 the Manchus retained their national costume and decreed that both Manchu and Chinese officials must wear Manchu style clothing. But in 1652 they adopted the Ming custom of using squares to indicate rank, and riding jackets with embroidered squares attached were worn by officials. The riding jacket opened down the front, so the front square was bisected, while the back square was in one piece.

The single bird of the late Ming squares was retained by the Qing as a typical heraldic symbol but was depicted in a stiff, unrealistic way. At the bottom of the square, a boulder, which served as a perch for the animal or bird, had waves at each side with some of the lucky symbols appearing out of the sea. These badges of the early Kangxi period, some of which were rich and gaudy reflecting the taste of the upstart owners, were smaller than those of the Ming and had a wide border with paired scrolls in gold. The background had irregular masses of laid gold thread around clouds and emblems, while peacock feathers, sent as tribute from Annam, were couched and used to add definition to both the boulder and the border. Later Kangxi badges had fewer clouds and straight laid gold couching which was attached with small vertical stitches to give a woven appearance.

The sun disk made its appearance on civil squares towards the end of the seventeenth century, although it appeared much later on military squares. It was placed in an upper corner with the bird or animal looking up at it, a symbol of the official looking up to his emperor. The sun disk, sometimes made of small coral beads, was very significant and always densely embroidered, and even when the squares were much simplified in the last ten years of the dynasty, the sun was retained.

By the Yongzheng and early Qianlong periods the squares had become less gaudy, and had more subdued backgrounds and very narrow borders with the symbols of rank properly emphasized.

With the promulgation of *The Illustrated Guide to Ritual Paraphernalia* the laws for insignia badges were finalized, and remained unchanged until the end of the dynasty in 1911. Roundels worn by the imperial family had five-clawed dragons shown full-face for the higher ranks or in profile for the lower ranks. At this time too, the Qianlong emperor, who loved pomp and pageantry, added the first pair of the twelve imperial symbols to the roundels on his *pufu*. These two symbols (sun and moon) were added to the two shoulder roundels, while the roundels on the chest and back had the *shou* character. Later, towards the end of the nineteenth century, squares with hoofed dragons appeared, presumably for lower-ranking noblemen not entitled to wear the clawed dragons.

In the middle of the Qianlong period there was a return to a more natural style of decoration in the mandarin squares. The smaller bird or animal was shown among trees and flowers, and the symbols disappeared. But then a period of degeneration followed as the weaker emperors imposed fewer constraints. The squares gradually became smaller and appeared to become just decorative patches, providing a place for lucky symbols, such as the long life symbols of *lingzhi*, pine, and peach. For despite the Manchu insistence on enforcing their customs and dress, many Chinese symbolic motifs were used both on the rank badges and on other costume. During the nineteenth century, the squares were crowded with more and more of these symbols, in particular those of the Eight Immortals and the Eight Buddhist Emblems.

Although it had always been possible for a man to purchase a degree, and consequently a rank, to become a member of the lower gentry, this trend increased rapidly towards the end of the Qing dynasty as from 1843 the government began selling ranks to generate revenue. Ranks without office began to be sold, even to merchants and tradesmen, and a man could buy a rank for himself, his father and sometimes even his deceased ancestors. He could also buy a rank without office in order to wear the rank badge and hat with the corresponding button. This led to the practice of wearing appliquéd birds and animals instead of those embroidered into the square. This meant that when the official rose with speed through the ranks, the base could be retained and just the bird changed. It also meant that one could select a background square made by the shop and then choose the sun, and the bird or animal to be added to left or right for the man and his wife.

During the nineteenth century the waves at the bottom of the square were raised by five to eight centimetres and slanting lines to represent the deep sea were added. Known as *lishui*, this design echoed the lower hem decoration which had been on the dragon robes from the middle of the eighteenth century. The background became fuller, either with all-over patterns of vine tendrils or key-fret design, or else filled completely with couched gold thread placed horizontally. The need for variety also brought back the *kesi* technique.

The borders, which had been narrow key-fret patterns of couched gold thread, now became more elaborate, and were often a vine pattern with small flowers at intervals, or else stylized dragons chasing a flaming pearl or long life character. The idea of placing lucky symbols in borders gained ground and a design of bats and the character *shou* was very common at the end of the nineteenth century. Also aniline dyes, imported from the West from the 1870s onwards, were harsh and unnatural and changed the look of the squares considerably. Finally some were even made circular, a serious breach of tradition as the circle was always reserved for the emperor and his immediate family.

In 1898 the young Guangxu emperor was persuaded to announce a series of decrees aimed at the modernization of all aspects of government, including the civil service examinations. This period, known as the Hundred Days of Reform, was short-lived, but the change spread to the badges of rank, which, in reaction to all the previous elaboration, became very simple. Those from the early part of the twentieth century showed only the animal or flying bird against a cloud-filled sky, though some still retained the Eight Buddhist symbols arranged in a circle around it. Others however continued to become more and more garish so that most of the square was embroidered with couched gold thread with contrasting colours of thread, often red and green, to secure the gold thread.

Women's Badges

Where badges were concerned the rank of a Qing official extended to his wife or wives and unmarried sons and daughters. At first the squares were identical, but around the middle of the eighteenth century the custom began of depicting the wife's bird or animal facing the opposite direction to that of her husband's, so that when they sat together in state, with the wife at the left of her husband as they faced the onlookers, the animals or birds would be facing each other. Later on, the badges were made even more distinct with the embroidery done in such a way as to form a circle inside the square.

Ancestor Portraits

The idea of facing birds is well displayed on ancestor portraits which were painted posthumously, and hung in the temple or altar room to be venerated at important anniversaries and weddings. The portraits were painted by artisans who would offer a selection of features from which the relatives chose those which most resembled the ancestor. The most important element of the portrait was the badge of rank, and often the *pufu* with the embroidered square was handed over to the painter so that the detail would be accurate.

Additional ancestor portraits were painted long after the subjects had died, to replace ones lost or burnt, or if the original portrait of a remote ancestor was in his village far from the current settlement of the clan. The details of the subject were unlikely to be accurate, and the painter's ignorance meant that Ming ancestors were often shown wearing Qing squares. Portraits were also painted to bolster up a newly created official or successful merchant, though in this case, the rank badge was often painted rather indistinctly. After the advent of the camera, the man and his wife were photographed for posterity wearing their official robes and the photograph hung in the altar room or temple for worship by their descendants.

Non-official Squares

Apart from insignia badges depicting the rank of noblemen and officials, other types of squares appeared from time to time. In Beijing, in the Ming and early Qing, musicians wore squares with the oriole bird, while officials who 'followed the plough' at the annual agricultural ceremony wore squares with a sun among clouds above a triple mountain.

Birthday squares with lavish floral designs were made as presents for family and friends. These were roughly the same size as the mandarin squares but instead of a bird or animal often featured chrysanthemums or peonies.

Four-character squares are often seen on ancestor portraits of elderly men who had attained no official rank, but who had celebrated their sixtieth or seventieth birthday. These squares are similar in appearance and size to a mandarin square, but in place of a bird or animal, the four large characters, *huang enqin zi* meaning 'conferred by imperial grace', are embroidered in couched gold thread on a black silk background. The square on the back has a large *shou* (long life) character in the centre, with a flying bat in each corner. Possibly these squares were bestowed on men who had been unable to hold an official position.

After the fall of the Qing dynasty in 1911, clothing gradually began to change. The dragon robe, symbol of imperial domination, was no longer worn, but the newly founded Republic of China determined that the *magua* and *changfu* become the official dress to be worn for sixtieth birthday celebrations, for successive birthdays, for important festivals and for burial.

Military squares were no longer worn; although civil squares

1. Front insignia square belonging to an imperial princess; embroidery on silk of four couched gold phoenix birds ascending and descending amid plum blossom and bamboo which, together with the two white rams, marks the winter solstice. Size 37 cm W. at base, 34 cm W. at top, 36 cm H.; Ming. (*Source*: private collection)

2. Imperial badge for the Lantern Festival: embroidered design of lantern and two dragons on silk, 36 cm diam.; Ming, Wanli period. (*Source*: private collection)

3. Lion for first or second rank military official; back square, *kesi*, size 38 cm W. × 35 cm H.; Ming. (*Source*: private collection)

4. Nobleman's front square of couched gold and silver thread depicting front-facing hoofed dragon; 31 cm W. × 30 cm H.; mid-nineteenth century. (*Source*: author's collection)

5 and 6. Pair of nineteenth-century ancestor portraits showing mandarin of fifth rank and his wife with facing birds; southern Guangdong. (*Source*: author's collection)

7. Ancestor portrait showing four-character square; nineteenth century. (*Source*: author's collection)

8. Back square worn for important birthday and ceremonial affairs, and also on burial robes; couched gold and silver thread with floss silk embroidery on brown satin ground, 'ninth rank, paradise flycatcher', 23 cm W. × 23 cm H.; 1970s, Hong Kong. (*Source:* author's collection)

9. First civil rank — Crane. Back square, appliquéd bird of silver tent stitch on tent stitch background; sun missing; size 24 cm W. × 22.5 cm H.; late nineteenth century. (*Source*: author's collection)

10. Second civil rank — Golden Pheasant. Front square; tent stitch bird appliquéd on tent stitch key-fret background and eight Buddhist emblems; sun missing; size 29.5 cm sq; late nineteenth century. (*Source*: author's collection)

11. Third civil rank — Peacock. Back square; silk and swirling couched gold thread embroidery, couched peacock feathers; size 33.5 cm W. × 35.5 cm H.; early Kangxi period. (*Source*: Teresa Coleman Fine Arts, Hong Kong)

12. Fourth civil rank — Cloud Goose. Back square; appliquéd bird on couched silk embroidery with seed stitch narcissi; size 23.5 cm W. × 21.5 cm H.; mid-nineteenth century. (*Source*: author's collection)

13. Fifth civil rank − Silver Pheasant. Front square; brick stitch and florentine stitch, appliquéd bird inside circle with eight Buddhist emblems, no border, women's style; size 25 cm W. × 23.5 cm H.; late nineteenth century. (*Source*: author's collection)

14. Sixth civil rank − Egret. Front square; couched gold thread with seed stitch clouds, bird and *lishui*; size 29 cm W. × 26.5 cm H.; early nineteenth century. (*Source*: author's collection)

15. Seventh civil rank — Mandarin Duck. Front roundel; *kesi* design of bats, swastika, and four of the emblems of the Eight Immortals; size 28.5 cm diam.; late nineteenth century. (*Source*: author's collection)

16. Eighth civil rank — Quail. Back square; brick stitch and florentine stitch with appliquéd bird in couched thread; size 30 cm W. × 29 cm H.; late nineteenth century. (*Source*: author's collection)

17. Ninth civil rank – Paradise Flycatcher. Back square, seed stitch mountains and clouds, couched gold thread bird on satin background; size 27.5 cm sq.; Qianlong style. (*Source*: private collection)

18. Censor – *Xiezhi*. Brick and florentine stitch with a key-fret background worked on gauze, size 24 cm W. × 22 cm H.; mid-nineteenth century. (*Source*: collection of Judith Rutherford)

19. First military rank − *Qilin*. Back square of straight laid couched gold thread background with couched peacock feather rock, satin stitch animal; size 24 cm W. × 23 cm H.; late Kangxi period. (*Source*: collection of Judith Rutherford)

20. Second military rank − Lion. Front square, *kesi*, natural style with animal amid swirling clouds on mountain with pavilion at right; size 26 cm sq.; Qianlong period. (*Source*: 950.100.316 Krenz Collection. Gift of Mrs Sigmund Samuel; photo courtesy of the Royal Ontario Museum, Toronto, Canada)

21. Third military rank — Leopard. Back square with appliquéd animal; satin stitch embroidery; size 23.5 cm W. × 22cm H.; late nineteenth century. (*Source*: collection of Judith Rutherford)

22. Fourth military rank — Tiger. Front square; satin stitch with couched outline; character for 'king' on head; size 30 cm W. × 28 cm H.; Reform style, early twentieth century. (*Source*: author's collection)

23. Fifth military rank − Bear. Back square; *kesi* with emblems of the Eight Immortals; size 30.5 cm W. × 29 cm H.; mid–nineteenth century (*Source*: author's collection)

24. Sixth and/or seventh military rank − Panther. Front square; couched gold and silver thread; appliquéd animal and sun; size 31 cm W. × 29.5 cm H.; late nineteenth century. (*Source*: author's collection)

continued they were made without any individuality. They had a simple border, *lishui* and rocks with the bird embroidered into the badge and not, as previously, applied separately. In the New Territories of Hong Kong, important clan members continued to wear a rank badge. These squares were often very crudely embroidered and there was no attempt to depict different birds as there had been previously. The symbolism of birds and animals no longer played any part in the hierarchy of officialdom.

6

Civil Squares

THE nine ranks of civil officials were each depicted by a different bird (see table below). Why a particular bird was chosen to represent a rank is not known. However, a Ming statesman, Qin Xun, suggests in his writings that birds symbolize the literary refinement of scholars, and animals, depicted on the military squares, the courage of the military. Furthermore, the ability of birds to fly up to heaven made the civil mandarins superior to the military mandarins symbolized by earth-bound animals.

For the collector, matching pairs of squares for the mandarin and his wife are very desirable items. Certain civil ranks were more numerous than others, and as can be expected there are a limited number of squares of the first and second rank. Squares of the fifth rank appear to outnumber those of the sixth to eighth ranks, and so must have been worn by a much larger proportion of officials. Ninth rank badges, dating from the years after the founding of the Republic, are common as they were worn by minor officials and selected village elders.

Rank	Early Ming (1391–1527)	Late Ming (1527–1644)	Qing (1652–1911)
First	crane or	crane	crane
Second	golden pheasant	golden pheasant	golden pheasant
Third	peacock or	peacock	peacock
Fourth	wild goose	wild goose	wild goose
Fifth	silver pheasant	silver pheasant	silver pheasant
Sixth	egret or	egret	egret
Seventh	mandarin duck	mandarin duck	mandarin duck
Eighth	oriole or	oriole	quail
Ninth	quail or	quail	paradise flycatcher
Unclassed officials	paradise flycatcher	paradise flycatcher	—

Source: Cammann 1952.

The following paragraphs list the birds and their descriptions as an aid to identification. There are various reasons why it is sometimes difficult to distinguish between the different birds. Firstly, it is unlikely that the embroiderer had seen the subject matter live, and would be

40

relying on doubtful representations for guidance. Secondly, unscrupulous officials would try to have their rank symbol embroidered to resemble that of the rank above. Edicts were repeatedly issued by the emperors to curtail this deviousness. In addition, towards the end of the dynasty all the birds were also depicted in gold and silver threads rendering colour useless as a means of identification.

The crane (*xianhe*) represents the first rank. It is a symbol of longevity as Chinese mythology gave a 2,000 year life span to the white Manchurian crane. After this time it was said to turn completely black. It is shown as a white bird with a black or red head, a long neck sometimes with a black patch, and short tail plumes. The feathers on the body are often in a scale pattern.

The golden pheasant (*jinji*) represents the second rank. It is shown as a brightly coloured bird often with a blue crest, yellow head and neck, and red lower legs and beak. Its distinctive tail had two straight parallel plumes, lightly barred in black. Early Qing golden pheasants sometimes have three or more wavy tail feathers with bars.

The peacock (*kongqiao*) represents the third rank. It is shown by small green feathers on the head and a spreading green tail with plumes bearing a characteristic eye.

The wild goose (or cloud goose) (*yunyan*) represents the fourth rank. It is shown with a light tan rectangular head, wing covers and back, with the front of the neck and breast sometimes in paler tan. It has a black or grey patch under its chin and paired comma marks in black on the upper head and back.

The silver pheasant (*baixian*) represents the fifth rank. It is shown on Ming squares as a white bird with a blue or green crest and from two to five long tail plumes with shorter ones at the base. In Qing times it was all white with five widely separated scalloped tail plumes.

The egret (*lisi*) represents the sixth rank, and is shown as a white bird with a very short tail, prominent crest feathers and light green or yellow bill and legs.

The mandarin duck (*qizhi*) represents the seventh rank. It is brightly coloured but usually predominantly blue. The colouring was decided by the maker but usually it had a blue back with feathers in a scale pattern, a short blue tail with feathers gathered in a wedge shape curving upwards at the end, a red bill and legs, and a yellow neck with long narrow feathers in two tiers.

The quail (*anxun*) represents the eighth rank, and is shown as a plump bird with short wings and a very little tail with pointed feathers at the base. It is usually coloured brown or mustard with a lighter breast; the all over scale pattern of its overlapping feathers is very distinctive.

The oriole (*huangli*) also represents the eighth or ninth rank, for Ming officials only. However it was also used on a small scale for musicians in Beijing during the Qing period. The very few surviving examples show a small long-tailed bird in yellow with back, wing covers, and tail lightly marked in black.

The paradise flycatcher (*lianqiao*) represents the ninth rank. It was shown on Ming squares as a white bird with a prominent crest and two long tail plumes. The Qing and twentieth-century ones had broader tail feathers at the ends, marked with a large dot. The crest was in blue or matched the tail colour.

One further badge worn by officials with civil responsibilities, but not included in the nine civil ranks was that of the censor. The censor's role was to report on the honesty and integrity of the other mandarins. Unlike the civil badges this had an animal depicted on it similar to the *baize* worn by second rank Ming noblemen. This animal was the *xiezhi*, a mythical white monster with a solid coloured body without scales, a green mane and a bushy tail. It had only one horn and two long whiskers. It was thought to be able to tell right from wrong, and to use its horn to gore the wrongdoer.

7
Military Squares

THE Manchus had for long been famous as a race of warriors whose banners or troops were feared as invincible throughout Asia. But towards the end of their reign over the conquered Chinese their powers diminished. The lasting peace had made the Manchu conquerors ineffectual and indifferent to incidents of disorder or revolt.

Officials employed in the army wore badges on which an animal depicted their rank. These military squares are limited in number and not easy to acquire, for unlike the civil ranks whose squares could be purchased towards the end of the dynasty, military positions were prized by the Manchu army. It is unlikely that ranks were sold to the conquered Chinese. Furthermore, upper-class Chinese, who were hostile to the Manchu military, would not have coveted these squares which were only worn by troops stationed in the provincial garrisons and in Manchu quarters in the larger cities.

When the Revolution overturned the Qing dynasty in 1911, the provincial garrisons were the first places to be attacked. Military officials, afraid of being recognized, burnt their squares and other marks of identification. Furthermore, these badges were of no value in the new government, whereas the civil officials often backed the new regime in the hope of keeping their property intact.

Rank	Ming (1391–1644)	Early Qing (1652–	Late Qing –1911)
First	lion	lion	qilin (after 1662)
Second	lion	lion	lion
Third	tiger and/or	tiger	leopard (after 1664)
Fourth	leopard	leopard	tiger (after 1664)
Fifth	bear	bear	bear
Sixth	panther	panther	panther
Seventh	panther	panther	rhinoceros (after 1759)
Eighth	rhinoceros	rhinoceros	rhinoceros
Ninth	sea-horse	sea-horse	sea-horse

Source: Cammann 1952.

Animals used on military squares were mythical, as shown by the use of the flame motifs that usually surrounded the beast. They were often embroidered without any attempt to obtain a true likeness. The following paragraphs contain a description of these animals.

Fig. 7.1. Seventh and/or eighth military rank — Rhinoceros, *kesi*. Brownish animal with black spots; fragment (detail), size 15 cm W. × 14 cm H., Ming. (*Source*: The Metropolitan Museum of Art, Rogers Fund, 1932. (32.111.2) All rights reserved, The Metropolitan Museum of Art, New York)

Fig. 7.2. Ninth military rank — Sea-horse. Red and yellow tent stitch on gauze; size 34 cm sq, early eighteenth century. (*Source*: The Metropolitan Museum of Art, Fletcher Fund, 1941. (41.123.3) All rights reserved, The Metropolitan Museum of Art, New York)

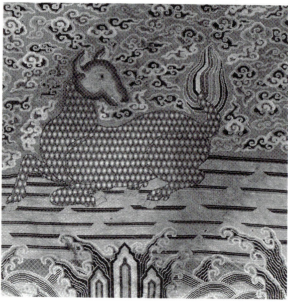

The *qilin* represents the first rank. It is often to be found in Chinese art and mistakenly called a unicorn by Western writers. It is a composite beast, with a dragon's head, a pair of horns, hooves, the body of a stag covered with large blue or green scales, and a bushy lion's tail. It was thought to be very wise.

The *baize* represents the second rank, and was only worn by Ming noblemen. It is a white creature resembling a lion, with rough scales on its shoulder and flank, without hooves, and depicted on Ming squares with two horns. It was no longer used during the Qing dynasty.

The lion (*shizi*) represents the second rank, and resembled the Buddhist 'snow lion' in late Qing. It was a large white animal with a green curly mane, back crest, and bushy tail. Earlier examples had a blue body.

The leopard (*bao*) represents the third rank, and bore the closest resemblance to a live animal except at the end of the dynasty when the spots became faint circles. Sometimes it had a circular star with radiating lines on its forehead.

The tiger (*hu*) represents the fourth rank. It is often mentioned together with the leopard in the Ming regulations, the former to represent the male and the latter the female. It also resembled a living animal with the stripes correctly depicted, until the end of the Qing dynasty when the stripes became comma-shaped lines. It often had the character for king (王) on its brow.

The bear (*xiongba*) represents the fifth rank. It bore no resemblance to the living animal being depicted with a blue body, green mane, bushy tail and white paws. It is easily confused with the lion, except in later Qing examples, when its mane was straight and the lion's curly.

The panther represents the sixth and/or seventh rank. It was sometimes called a tiger cat (*biao*) and shown as a yellowish cat-like animal with a white chest. It had no distinguishing markings.

The rhinoceros (*xiniu*) represents the seventh and/or eighth rank. It was in fact a completely mythical creature better described as the Chinese unicorn. It was like a cow with a large horn on the back of the head, curling forward between the ears, and a long thin tail (see Fig. 7.1).

The sea-horse (*haima*) represents eighth rank. It was not a curling sea-horse, but the legendary horse of the sea. It is extremely rare, as examples of this lowly ninth rank would have belonged to provincial soldiers who would have had to destroy them in 1911 (see Fig. 7.2).

8
Symbolism Used on the Rank Badges

T H E Manchus began their rule by insisting that their costume and customs be adopted by the conquered race. Continual edicts were imposed on the Chinese officials to make sure that the Han Chinese pattern and style of dress did not infiltrate. But as the reign progressed, there was a gradual adoption by the Manchu court and officials of Chinese pictorial emblems, especially those depicting wealth, health, and happiness.

The trend of using Chinese symbols began on Manchu informal clothing, but spread to official badges of rank during the late eighteenth century. The symbols to fill in the background of the badges were used increasingly towards the end of the nineteenth century. This was a time of uncertainty, when many propitious symbols were used to invoke favourable spiritual powers, and by the end of the dynasty Chinese nature symbolism had been completely accepted by the Manchus.

Symbolism plays an important role in the folklore of most societies, with certain objects or species being endowed with protective or propitious properties. The Chinese language has many homophones and many things are used as propitious symbols because the word sounds the same as something which is considered lucky. This resulted in verbal puns displayed as rebuses with pictorial symbols, and showed a high level of literary taste.

The Symbols

The following paragraphs list the common patterns and motifs endowed with symbolic meaning and which were frequently used to form the background and border of the badge of rank.

Bamboo stands for longevity, courage in adversity, and for winter. It stays green in the cold weather and keeps its leaves long after other plants have lost theirs. It is a popular symbol for mandarins because its straight growth represented an honest and uncorrupt official. It is also one of the four noble plants.

The bat is a popular symbol as *fu* (bat) sounds similar to *fu* (happiness). Five bats shown together signify the five blessings: longevity, health, wealth, virtue, and the right to a natural death. Bats were frequently used around the border of the square.

The butterfly is an old and very common symbol standing for great age because the name *tie* sounds like the word for seventy or eighty years of age. The butterfly also represents the summer.

The chrysanthemum is one of the four important flower emblems and is one of the four noble plants. It stands for autumn, and contented middle age. It also represents friendship.

Coins symbolize wealth.

Stylized clouds were a symbol of heaven and long life and appeared endlessly on dragon robes and badges. They were useful as space fillers and to unify a design.

The dragon is the symbol of imperial authority. The five-clawed *long* dragon was reserved for the emperor and members of his immediate family. The four-clawed *mang* dragon was for lesser nobles and those who had had the honour conferred upon them.

The fish is the emblem of wealth and abundance, since the homophone (*yu*) means superfluity. Owing to its reproductive powers it is also the symbol of regeneration and, because it is happy in its natural habitat, symbolizes harmony with nature.

Stylized flames often surrounded the animals on the badges to indicate their mythical and mystical nature. They are also used extensively on dragon robes to symbolize fire and consuming energy.

There were twelve imperial symbols which originated in the *Book of Rites* and were described in a memorial on regulations for official costumes in the *Kangxi Encyclopaedia*. The first two symbols, for sun and moon, were added by the Qianlong emperor to the roundels on the *pufu* worn by the emperor and high-ranking princes.

The lotus is a symbol of purity, fruitfulness, perfection. It is one of the four important flower emblems representing summer, and an important motif in Chinese art which also represented Buddha. It had almost the same significance as the cross has in Christianity, as it is the emblem of redemption and purity: it grows out of mud but its blossom is undefiled. The lotus flower with the egret symbolizes the honesty of an uncorrupt official, as the bird keeps its white plumage clean even in the dirty water of a lotus pond.

The magnolia represents the spring, while mountains are a symbol of earth, steadfastness and longevity. Mountains are one of the elements of the cosmos when used on the dragon robe, together with *lishui*.

The narcissus is a sign of winter and of the Lunar New Year, while the orchid is one of the four noble plants. peach blossom represents the spring, is an emblem of marriage, and a symbol of immortality, while the peach also represents springtime and is one of the ten long-life symbols. It is said to be the food of life, especially of the Eight Immortals.

The peony is another of the four flower emblems signifying summer, wealth and honour. It was also a hope for greater advancement and often used alone.

The phoenix is an ancient figure signifying goodness and benevolence, and was used to symbolize the empress of China. A pair of phoenixes on a badge of rank for princesses and lesser noblewomen represented the male (*feng*) and female (*huang*) principle. The pine is one of the ten longevity symbols; an evergreen, and hence a symbol of long life, strength and vitality. The plum blossom, the last of the four flower emblems, symbolizes winter and beauty and is one of the four noble plants. It also symbolizes immortality because the blossom appears on leafless branches. It is shown with pine and bamboo to form a trio called 'the three friends in winter', representing loyal companions in times of stress. The pomegranate, with its many seeds, symbolizes abundance. The rose is the flower of lasting springtime and enduring youth. The sacred fungus (*lingzhi*) gives eternal life if eaten and is one of the ten longevity symbols.

Shou is the character for long life which often appeared in the border design around the square. When combined with the bat motif or swastika pattern it stood for long life and happiness. The sun is a symbol of heaven and the emperor, and intellectual enlightenment. The swastika pattern (*wan*) is one of the oldest designs in the world, and is said to have been associated with prehistoric shaman rituals. It became a Buddhist lucky symbol around AD 200 and represents the seal of Buddha's heart. It is often incorporated into a design with *shou* to mean 'ten thousand years of long life'.

The thunder line is another prehistoric emblem dating from the Shang dynasty or before. It is so called because it resembles the ancient Chinese character for thunder. It is often used as a border design, sometimes with the swastika motif.

The Four Attributes of the Scholar are books, scroll paintings, the lute and the chess-board. These were popular in the nineteenth century as they represented to the beleaguered officials the leisurely life of contemplation which they hoped was to follow in retirement (see Fig. 8.1).

The Eight Buddhist Emblems shown in Fig. 8.2 are also called the 'eight lucky things' (*ba ji xiang*). These are the wheel of the law, a symbol of Buddhist teaching which leads the disciple to Nirvana, the conch shell, originally used to call the faithful to prayer, and a Buddhist symbol of victory; the umbrella, a symbol of nobility which sheds the heat of desire; the canopy, a symbol of victory over the religions of the world; the lotus, a symbol of purity and promise of Nirvana; the jar, also called the 'treasury of all desires', and said to contain the elixir of heaven; a pair of fish representing happiness and the symbol of *yin* and *yang*, the female and male principle respectively, signifying a balance of opposites in nature; and the endless knot, symbol of the Buddhist path and the 'thread' which guides one to happiness.

Fig. 8.1. The Four Attributes of the Scholar. From the left: the chess-board, a lute, books, and scroll paintings. (*Source*: Chavannes 1973)

Wheel of the Law   Conch Shell

Umbrella   Canopy

Lotus   Jar

Fish   Endless Knot

Fig. 8.2. The Eight Buddhist Emblems. (*Source*: Burkhardt 1955–9)

The Eight Taoist Emblems, shown in Fig. 8.3, are carried by the Eight Immortals who are the Taoist patron saints. These emblems are the fan (delicacy of feeling), a symbol of Zhongli Chuan, patron saint of the military; the sword (superhuman power), a symbol of Lu Dongbiu, a scholar-warrior and patron of barbers; the gourd (medicine), with the crutch, the symbol of Li Dieguai the patron saint of the sick; castanets (music), symbol of Cao Guochui, patron saint of actors; the flower basket (long life), a symbol of Lan Caihou, patron of gardeners and florists. The bamboo tube and rods (long life), were a symbol of Zhang Guolao, patron saint of artists and calligraphers; the flute (harmony), a symbol of Han Xiangzi, patron saint of musicians; and the lotus (purity), a symbol of Hou Xiangu, the female patron saint of housewives.

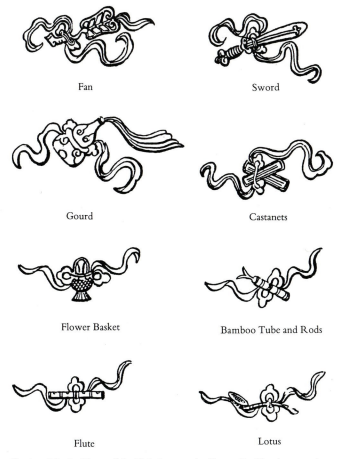

Fan

Sword

Gourd

Castanets

Flower Basket

Bamboo Tube and Rods

Flute

Lotus

Fig. 8.3. The Emblems of the Eight Immortals. (*Source*: Burkhardt 1955–9)

The Eight Precious Things (*ba bao*) were also known as Eight Treasures. They were the pearl representing good fortune, the coin representing wealth, the lozenge representing victory, the mirror representing conjugal happiness, the stone chime representing happiness, books representing wisdom, rhinoceros horn cups representing health, the artemesia leaf representing happiness. They are illustrated in Fig. 8.4.

The Pearl   Coin

Lozenge   Mirror

Stone Chime   Books

Rhinoceros Horns   Artemesia Leaf

Fig. 8.4. The Eight Treasures. (*Source*: Burkhardt 1955–9)

9
Methods of Making the Badges

INSIGNIA badges from the Ming dynasty were often made of brocade, whose homophone *jin* means 'gold' or 'money'. Popular in China since the Han dynasty (206BC–AD220), brocade reached its peak of popularity in the Song dynasty when it became possible to weave very naturalistic landscape designs into the fabric. It was in demand in the Ming dynasty for badges of rank, on which the vigorous patterns show swirling clouds around the animal or bird with turbulent waves below.

However, *kesi* designs were more plentiful during the Ming period and reached a high degree of excellence. *Kesi*, or cut silk, was the name for a silk tapestry weave where vertical slits occurred when one colour ended and the next began. The undyed warp threads were woven with coloured weft threads, each colour covering only the area of its own pattern. Fine detail was sometimes added in ink, this being more common when this weave technique was revived during the middle of the nineteenth century.

The majority of the insignia badges from the Qing dynasty were embroidered on to a base cloth of silk gauze or satin. The disruption at the beginning of the dynasty of the silk-weaving industry in Yangzhou and the other manufacturing cities was responsible for this change and led to a variety of other techniques being employed. Where silk was used, it was used sparingly. An examination of the backs of the badges shows that there are no floating threads, unlike later in the Qianlong period when floats across the different colours were much longer.

The embroidery thread used was generally floss silk or less often twisted silk. Floss silk gave a glossy effect and was mostly used for filling spaces, as it gave an impression of light and shade when the direction of the stitch was changed. Great care, however, had to be taken when working with the floss threads so that they would not become fluffy or uneven. In the early Qing even couched peacock feathers were incorporated into the design of the rock on which the bird or animal was standing and also into the border of the square.

In the later years of the dynasty in the Guangxu period much use was made of laid gold thread, couched on to satin in order to economize on silk, as well as to give the desired rich and gaudy effect. The threads were said to have a special coating which prevented them from tarnishing in hot and humid weather, and this secret had long been highly sought after outside China. In Sir George Staunton's account of Lord Macartney's embassy to China in 1793–4, it is said that an English manufacturer by the name of Eades accompanied the embassy in order to discover the secret of this coating. Unfortunately, however, Eades was not successful in his quest as he contracted an illness on the outward journey and died soon after his arrival in China. In fact, a description of the method of manufacturing gold and silver thread, written nearly three-quarters of a century later, makes no mention of the special coating:

Several long, and narrow sheets of paper having been coated with a mixture of earth (well pounded) and glue are, in the next instance, covered either with gold, or silver leaf. In order that a bright glossy appearance may be imparted to these sheets of paper, which, with gold, or silver leaf have been covered, men rub them, heavily, from one end to the other, with pieces of crystal, which, for this purpose, are, to the ends of the bamboo rods, attached. This polishing process having been accomplished, the gilded, or silvered sheets of paper are, now, cut, by means of large knives, into very thin strips, which strips, are, then, by a twirling process, carefully entwined round ordinary threads of silk. (Gray 1875)

Embroidery Stitches

The repertoire of stitches was not large, and often the badge was embroidered using a very limited number of stitch types. The following list gives the most common ones empoled. Fig. 9.1 illustrates these stitches.

BRICK STITCH

This is a flat satin stitch used in a staggered sequence to give an interesting textured effect when filling large areas.

COUCHING

Gold and silver threads were used to outline a design and as a means of providing additional texture. Metal thread could not be sewn directly as it would be very likely to break. It was therefore laid in rows on the surface of the cloth and a toning silk thread was employed to anchor it in position. Later red and green silk were used for this purpose, since it was thought that these colours enhanced the colour of the metal. It was common by the end of the nineteenth century and the beginning of the twentieth century for the whole of the embroidered design to be made of couched metal thread.

FLORENTINE STITCH

This stitch was worked with silk thread on canvas ground. Vertical parallel straight stitches rise or descend according to the pattern being followed. Often, each line is worked in a shade or colour different from the one before.

LONG AND SHORT STITCH

This is a variation of satin stitch which is made by making the first row of stitches alternately long and short; thereafter all the rows have stitches the same length. This stitch is used to give gradations of colour and shade.

PEKINESE STITCH

This stitch was also called couched twist and is formed when a back stitch is interlaced with a looped second thread.

SATIN STITCH

Examples of this stitch were found in Shang tombs, dating from the sixteenth century BC to the eleventh century BC. This stitch became an important part of an embroiderer's repertoire in the Qing dynasty. The stitches should be very flat and even to give the characteristic satin-smooth appearance. Voiding, leaving a hair's breadth of fabric between adjacent areas of satin stitch, was very popular as a means of giving definition to the design.

SEED STITCH

This was also called Peking knot, and was similar to the French knot. Known as *dazi* in Chinese, or sometimes blind stitch due to the fact that the embroiderer could become blind embroidering such a small and even stitch. It was said to have been forbidden because of this risk, though there is no legal evidence of such a ban. The stitch was used to give a soft texture, to fill in small areas, or to define details. The stitches had to be absolutely even, next to each other, and the rows completely straight.

STEM STITCH

This stitch was used to outline a design and for fine detailing.

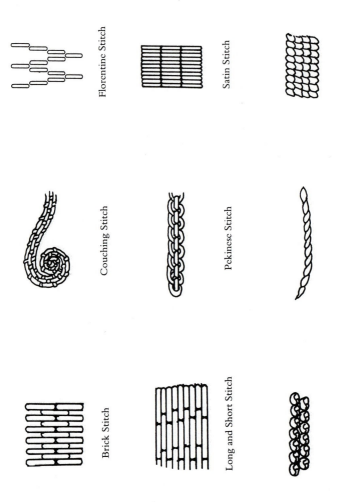

Florentine Stitch

Satin Stitch

Tent Stitch

Couching Stitch

Pekinese Stitch

Stem Stitch

Brick Stitch

Long and Short Stitch

Seed Stitch

Fig. 9.1. Embroidery stitches used on badges.

TENT STITCH

This stitch was also called half-cross stitch; it is a short, straight slanted stitch, used on an open weave cloth like canvas or gauze and good for covering a large area of background. Together with half-cross stitch, sometimes called *gros point*, these stitches are often erroneously referred to as tapestry.

Embroidery Designs

The task of embroidering the rank badges was sometimes undertaken at home by the wives and daughters of the mandarins, but it would more usually fall to a professional embroidery studio which often specialized in only one of the many designs. As the design of the insignia badge became more elaborate in the nineteenth century with the use of much pattern and symbolism, books of embroidery designs were consulted for the background, in which approved styles of embroidery and the arrangement of colours and patterns were set out. Rice paper cuts, made to be pasted on to the paper windows found in most Chinese homes, were also used as a base for design. Outlines of designs were marked with a thin line of black ink, or the edge of the paper design was sewn round as an outline and the paper ripped out. Another method entailed the use of a white powder made of ground oyster shells dusted through a stencil, leaving a powdery outline. More powder was mixed with water and a fine line painted over the outline to render it more permanent. The design was then embroidered.

Stencils of the most popular designs and symbols were made, and most large studios had a selection of cardboard templates which were used to give uniformity of design, and to assist in the placing of the design, as well as to save time. All the popular symbols such as the *shou* character, *fu*, key-fret, clouds, and common Buddhist and Taoist emblems were made this way.

Dyes

Until the middle of the nineteenth century almost all dyes came from plants, and are thus known as vegetable dyes. The base cloth, and the embroidery threads used were dyed according to the chosen colour with such plants as indigo (*indigofera tinctoria*) to give blue, and gall nuts or acorns for black. Yellow was produced from safflowers (*carthamus tinctorus*), and a mordant of potash could be added to the yellow juice to give a red dye. Green was produced by first dyeing blue, then overdyeing with yellow. Often the yellow has faded to leave a blue tint where once there was a green one. Purple was produced from a mixture of red and blue, and during the Jiaqing reign a rather bright violet shade made its appearance. Possibly produced from gromwell roots (*lithospermum crythrorhizon*), it nevertheless differed greatly from the purple of the aniline dyes, Perkin's violet, which were first invented in England in 1856.

These aniline dyes did not reach China until the 1870s, but immediately became popular and the vivid shades even appeared on the robes and squares made for the imperial family (Cammann 1979). Great use was made of these dyes on the insignia badges for the lower-ranking mandarins, and the bright and gaudy pinks, purples and greens are very common towards the end of the nineteenth century and in the twentieth century.

Conclusion

COMPARED with painting and porcelain from China, textiles and embroidery have not in the past received the attention from the scholar and collector they rightly deserved. Long hours were spent in the manufacture of each item, which was often unique and required great skill on the part of the worker.

In recent years, however, recognition has gradually been accorded to this significant area of Chinese cultural artefacts. Rank badges have now started to become important collectors' items, to the extent that in recent months, careful copies of squares made in China are appearing in antique shops. They are at present sold as copies, but it may not be long before they are being passed off to the unwary collector as originals. All those seen so far have been back squares, and naturally there have been many identical ones. A clue to their recent manufacture lies in the satin stitch embroidery which is not quite as even as on the originals. More noticeable is the sun which is quite sketchily embroidered and not as dense as it ought to be.

Dating rank badges, along with all items of Chinese dress, is one of the most difficult aspects of its study. Knowledge of the trends which arose, the colours which were restricted and others which were introduced helps in the dating. But confusion often occurs because old stylistic details were at times revived to give the square the appearance of greater antiquity, birds and animals were deliberately misrepresented to give the impression of a higher rank, and styles and symbols originally restricted to the imperial family became common property and were used by low-ranking officials.

In recent years, a number of Ming badges have appeared on the market. Many of these have come via Tibet where they were taken during the sixteenth and seventeenth centuries. Formed into *sutra* covers, banners and hangings for the temples and monasteries, they have been preserved in a state close to the original by the climatic conditions. An in-depth study of more of these very early badges will be welcomed. Information on rank badges given here is inevitably far from complete and can serve only as an introduction to the subject.

Glossary

TERMS are given in the *pinyin* romanization of Chinese, with the Chinese characters in parentheses.

Ancha shisi (按察使司) (colloquial, *nietai*, 臬台)
Anxun (鵪鶉)
Baixian (白鷳)
Baize (白澤)
Bao (豹)
Bazong (把總)
Biao (彪)
Buzheng shisi (布政使司) (colloquial, *fantai*, 藩台)
Canjiang (參將)
Changfu (長服)
Chaofu (朝服)
Dajiao (打醮)
Dianshi (殿試)
Dusi (都司)
Fujiang (副將)
Guan (官)
Haima (海馬)
Hu (虎)
Huangli (黃鸝)
Huishi (會試)
Jiansheng (監生)
Jinji (錦雞)
Jinshi (進士)
Junxiu (俊秀)
Juren (舉人)
Kongqiao (孔雀)
Lianqiao (練鵲)
Lishui (立水)
Lisi (鷺鷥)
Magua (馬褂)

Pufu (補服)
Puzi (補子)
Qianzong (千總)
Qifu (麒服)
Qilin (麒麟)
Qizhi (鸂鶒)
Shengyuan (生員)
Shenshi (紳士)
Shizi (獅子)
Shou (壽)
Shoubei (守備)
Tidu (提督)
Tongsheng (童生)
Tongshi (童試)
Waiwei bazong (外委把總)
Waiwei qianzong (外委千總)
Wan (萬)
Wujinshi (武進士)
Wujuren (武舉人)
Wushengyuan (武生員)
Xianhe (仙鶴)
Xiangshi (鄉試)
Xiezhi (獬豸)
Xiniu (犀牛)
Xiongba (熊羆)
Xiucai (秀才)
Xunfu (巡撫) (colloquial *futai*, 撫台)
Youji (遊擊)
Yunyan (雲雁)
Zongbing (總兵)
Zongdu (總督) (colloquial, *zhitai*, 制台)

Appendix

Qing Dynasty, 1644–1911

Shunzhi	1644–61
Kangxi	1661–1722
Yongzheng	1723–35
Qianlong	1736–95
Jiaqing	1796–1820
Daoguang	1821–50
Xianfeng	1851–61
Tongzhi	1862–74
Guangxu	1875–1908
Xuantong	1909–11

Bibliography

Alexander, William (1805), *The Costume of China* (London).

Ball, J. Dyer (1925), *Things Chinese* (fifth edition, Kelly and Walsh, Shanghai).

Burkhardt, V.R. (1955–9), *Chinese Creeds and Customs*, vols. 1–3 (South China Morning Post, Hong Kong).

Cammann, Schuyler (1944–5), 'The Development of the Mandarin Square', *Harvard Journal of Asiatic Studies*, vol. 8, pp. 71–130.

—— (1952), *China's Dragon Robes* (Ronald Press, New York).

—— (1953), 'Ming Festival Symbols', *Archives of the Chinese Art Society of America*, vol. II, pp. 68–9.

—— (1979), *Costume in China, 1644 to 1912* (Philadelphia Museum of Art).

Chang Chung-li (1970), *The Chinese Gentry* (University of Washington Press, Seattle and London).

Chavannes, E., and Atwood, E. (1973), *The Five Happinesses, Symbolism in Chinese Popular Art* (Weatherill).

Doolittle, Rev. Justus (1895), *Social Life of the Chinese*, Vols I and II (Harper and Bros, New York).

Gray, J.H. (1875), *Walks in the City of Canton* (de Souza, Hong Kong).

Hardy, Rev. E.J. (1905), *John Chinaman at Home* (Unwin, London).

Hayes, J.W. (1962), 'The Pattern of Life in the New Territories in 1898', *Journal of the Hong Kong Branch of the Royal Asiatic Society*, vol. 2, pp. 75–102.

Hunter, W.C. (1911), *Bits of Old China*, 2nd ed. (Kelly and Walsh, Shanghai).

Ker, W.P. (1903), *List of the Higher Metropolitan and Provincial Authorities of China* (Kelly and Walsh, Shanghai).

Lai, T.C. (1970), *A Scholar in Imperial China* (Kelly and Walsh, Hong Kong).

Marsh, Robert M. (1961), *The Mandarins The Circulation of Elites in China, 1600–1900* (The Free Press of Glencoe).

Mason, George Henry (1804), *The Costume of China* (London).

Mayers, W.F. (1896), *The Chinese Government — A Manual of Chinese Titles*, 3rd ed. revised by G.M.H. Playfair (Kelly and Walsh, Shanghai).

Meadows, Thomas Taylor (1847), *Desultory Notes on the Government and Peoples of China ...* (London).

Mesny, W. (1905), *Mesny's Chinese Miscellany* (Shanghai).

Morse, H.B. (1908), *Trade and Administration of the Chinese Empire* (Kelly and Walsh, Shanghai).

Oriental Ceramic Society of Hong Kong (1986), *Art from the Scholar's Studio* (Hong Kong University Press, Hong Kong).

Reischauer, E.O., and Fairbank, J.K. (1960), *East Asia The Great Tradition* (Houghton Mifflin Company, Boston).

Sirr, H.S. (1849), *China and the Chinese* (W.S.Orr and Co., London).

Smith, A.H. (1894), *Chinese Characteristics* (Fleming H. Revell Company, New York).

Smith, Richard J. (1974), 'Chinese Military Institutions in the Mid-Nineteenth

Century 1850–1860', *Journal of Asian History*, vol. 8, no. 2 (Otto Harrassowitz, Wiesbaden).

Thompson, John (1899), *Travels in China* (Harper and Bros, New York).

Turner, J.A. (1894), *Kwang Tung or Five Years in South China* (republished by Oxford University Press, Hong Kong, 1982).

Vollmer, John E. (1977), *In the Presence of the Dragon Throne* (Royal Ontario Museum, Toronto).

——(1983), *Decoding Dragons* (University of Oregon Museum of Art, Eugene).

Weale, B.L. Putnam (1904), *Manchu and Muscovite* (Macmillan and Co. Ltd., London).

Williams, C.A.S. (1931), *Outlines of Chinese Symbolism and Art Motives* (Customs College Press, Peking).

Wilson, Verity (1986), *Chinese Dress* (Victoria and Albert Museum, London).

Wright, G.N. (1843), *China in a Series of Views*.

Young Yang Chung (1979), *The Art of Oriental Embroidery* (Scribners, New York).

Index

Page numbers in italics refer to Figures

accessories, 6, 27, 33
ancestor portraits, 37, 38

badges of rank, *21*, 22, 24 26, 28, 33, 34,
  35, 36, 37, 40, 43, 46, 59, 60
  borders, 34, 35, 36, 37, 38, 46, 48
  brocade, 53
  embroidered, 34, 35, 36, 37, 39, 57
  Guangxu style, 37, 53
  Jiaqing style, 58
  Kangxi style, 35
  kesi, 34, 35, 36, *44*, 53
  Ming, 33, 34, 35, 42, 43, *44*, 45, 53, 59
  non-official, 38
  Qianlong style, 35, 36, 53
  twentieth-century style, 38, 42, 58
  women's, 29, 31, *31*, 37, 48
  Yongzheng style, 35
  see also insignia and roundels
baize, 34, 42, 45, 60
bat motif, 37, 38, 46, 48, 57
bear, 43, 45, 60
Beijing, 1, 2, 3, 9, 10, 13, 15, 19, 29, 38, 42
birthday squares, *see* badges of rank, non-
  official
blue quill plume, 29
Board of War, 9, 11
boots, 6, 29
bound feet, 30, 32

Canton, *see* Guangzhou
cap finials, *16*, 28, 33, 36
changfu, 24, *25*, 26, *27*, 38, 60
chaofu, *see* court robe
Chengdu, 28
clothing, non-official, 19, 25
  formal, 19, *23*, 25
  informal, 19, 25, 26
  semi-formal, 19, 25, 26, *26*
clothing, official, 19
  formal, 19, *20*, 21
  informal, 19, 24, *25*
  semi-formal, 19, 22, *22*, *23*, 24

cloud goose, *see* wild goose
cloud motif, 23, 35, 38, 47, 53, 57
collars, *lingtou*, 25, *25*, 26
  piling, 21, *21*, 22, *22*, 25
  Chinese woman's, 31
cotton, 21, 24
court robe, 19, 20, *20*, 21, *21*, 23, *23*, 24, 31,
  60
crane, 40, 41, 60

Dajiao ceremony, 6, 60
district magistrate, 5, 13
dragon motif, 20, 21, 23, 24, 34, 37, 47
dragon robe, 22, *22*, 23, *23*, 24, 25, 33, 35,
  36, 38, 47, 60
dyes, 21, 56, 57, 58
  aniline, 37, 58

education, civil, 4, 5
  military, 9
egret, 40, 41, 47, 60
Eight Buddhist Emblems, the, 36, 37, 48,
  50, 57
Eight Immortals, the, 36, 47, 51
Eight Precious Things, the, 34, *52*, *52*
Eight Taoist Emblems, the, 51, *51*, 57
embroidery: couched metal thread, 33, 34,
  35, 53, 54, *56*
  designs, 57, *57*
  silk thread, 53, 57
  stitches, 54, 55, *56*, 57, 59
  see also badges of rank
emperor, 2, 9, 11, 13, 15, 19
  dress of, 19, 20, 21, 23, 33, 47
  see also imperial family
examination hall, 6, 6, *7*, 8
examinations, 3, 4, 6, 8, 9, 37, 60
  civil, 5
  military, 9

fantai, *see* financial controller
financial controller, 13, *16*, 60
fish motif, 47
flame motif, 43, 47
flower motifs, 38, 47, 48

Four Attributes of the Scholar, the, 48, *49*
Four Character squares, *see* badges of rank,
   non-official
fu, see bat motif
Fujian province, 32
'full dress', 22, *22*, 28
futai, see governor

gentry status, 3, 3 6, 60
girdle, 27
girdle clasp, 27, 2 8
golden pheasant, 40, 41, 60
governor, 10, 13, 14, *16*, 60
governor-general, *16*, 21, *see also* viceroy
graduate, 6
   metropolitan, 9, *12*, 60
   military metropolitan, 10, 60
   military provincial, 10, 60
   provincial, 6, *12*, 60
graduation ceremony, 6, 9
graduation dress, 6, 9
Green Standard Army, 9, 11, 13, 14
Guangdong province, 5, 15, 21, *31*, 32
Guangxi province, 6, 21
Guangxu emperor, 37
Guangzhou, 6, 6, 7

hairstyles, 2, 28, 3 0, 32
'half dress', 25, *26*
Hakka, 32
Han Chinese, 19, 43, 46
   dress, 19
   pattern, 46
   symbolism, 36, 46
Han Chinese women, 30, *31*
   clothing, non-official, 30, 31, *31*
Han dynasty, 53
Hanlin Academy, 9, 11, *12*
headwear, 36
   graduation hat, 6
   Manchu woman's headdress, 30, *30*, 32
   mandarin's summer hat, 26, 28
   mandarin's winter hat, 22, 26, 28
Hong Kong, 6, 14, *27*, 39

*Illustrated Catalogue of Ritual Paraphernalia
of the Qing Dynasty*, 19, 35
Imperial Army, 1
Imperial Chancery, 11
imperial family, 1, 2, 20, 21, 33, 47
imperial insignia, 3 3, 34, 35, 37, 47, 48, 58

insignia badges, 33, 34, 35, 38, 53; *see also*
   badges of rank
Inner Mongolia, 2

jinshi, see graduate, metropolitan
junxiu, see student
juren, see graduate, provincial

Kangxi Encyclopaedia, 47
key-fret pattern, 36, 57

leopard, 43, 45, 60
lion, 43, 45, 60
lishui, 23, 36, 39, 47, 60
long life symbols, 33, 36, 37, 47, 47, 48; *see
also shou, wan*

magua, 26, *27*, 60; *see also* riding jacket
Manchu, 1, 3, 19, 32
   army, 13, 43
   bannermen, 1, 13, 43
   costume, 2, 19, 23, 29, 35, 36, 46
   empire, 2
   language, 2, 19
Manchu women, 29
   non-official clothing, 29, *30*
   official clothing, 29
Manchuria, 1, 2
mandarin, 3, 11, 13, 17, 18, 28
   civil, 3, 11, 15, 29
   dress, 19, 20, 21; *see also* clothing,
    official and non-official
   duties, 11
   military, 3, 11, 14, 15, 29
   ranks of, 11, 14, *16*, 24, 40
   regulations of, 15
   salary of, 14, 15, *16*
   square, *see* badges of rank
mandarin chain, 29
mandarin duck, 40, 41, 60
military commander-in-chief, 14, 60
Ming dynasty, 1, 3, 13, 20, 33, 38, 40, 53
Mongols, 13, 33
mountain motif, 23, 38, 47

New Territories, 6, 39
nietai, see provincial judge
noblemen, 1
   insignia, 33, 34, 36, 38, 42, 45, 47
   robes, 21, 33
see also imperial family

oriole, 38, 40, 42, 60
Outer Mongolia, 2

panther, 43, 45, 60
paradise flycatcher, 40, 42, 60
peacock, 40, 41, 60
peacock feather plume, *12*, *22*, 28, 29
Peking knot, *see* embroidery stitches
phoenix, 34, 47
provincial judge, 13, *16*, 60
pufu, *see* surcoat
purchase of degrees and ranks, 3, 9, 11, *12*,
    36, 43, 60
puzi, *see* badges of rank

Qianlong emperor, 19, 35, 47
qifu, *see* dragon robe
qilin, 34, 43, 45, 60
Qin dynasty, 1
quail, 40, 41, 60

Reform period, 37
Republic of China, 32, 38
rhinoceros, 43, *44*, 45, 60
riding jacket, 19, 35,
roundels, 33, 35, 36, 37, 47; *see also* badges
    of rank

satin, 24, 28, 30, 53
sea horse, 43, *44*, 45, 60
Shandong province, 28
Shang dynasty, 48, 55
shoes, 30, 32
shou symbol, 34, 36, 37, 38, 48, 57, 60
Shunzhi emperor, 1
Sichuan, 28
silk, 20, 24, 25, 26, 38, 53
    gauze, 24, 53, 57
silver pheasant, 40, 41, 60
Six Boards, the, 11
skirt, 31

sleeveless vest, Han Chin
    Manchu woman's, 29
Song dynasty, 33, 53
student, 5, 8, 9, 60
    government, 5, 60
    military government,
surcoat, 22, *22*, 24, *25*, 2(
sun disk, 35, 59
swastika pattern, 48, 60
symbols, 23, 24, 34, 35,

Taiwan, 2
Tang dynasty, 3
thunder line pattern, 48
Tibet, 2, 59
tidu, *see* military comm:
tiger, 43, 45, 60
trousers, 31
Turkestan, 2

viceroy, 11, 13, 14, 15, 1
    governor-general
Victoria and Albert Mu

wan symbol, *see* swastik:
Wanli reign, 33
wife of mandarin, *18*, 2(
    Chinese and Manchu
wild goose, 40, 41, 60

xiezhi, 42, 60
Xinjiang, 2
xiucai, *see* student , gov«

yamen, 6, 14, 17, 18
Yangzhou, 53
Yuan dynasty, 53

zhitai, *see* viceroy
Zhou dynasty, 3

Four Attributes of the Scholar, the, 48, *49*
Four Character squares, *see* badges of rank, non-official
fu, see bat motif
Fujian province, 32
'full dress', 22, *22*, 28
futai, see governor

gentry status, 3, 36, 60
girdle, 27
girdle clasp, 27, 28
golden pheasant, 40, 41, 60
governor, 10, 13, 14, *16*, 60
governor-general, *16*, 21, *see also* viceroy
graduate, 6
    metropolitan, 9, *12*, 60
    military metropolitan, 10, 60
    military provincial, 10, 60
    provincial, 6, *12*, 60
graduation ceremony, 6, 9
graduation dress, 6, 9
Green Standard Army, 9, 11, 13, 14
Guangdong province, 5, 15, *21*, *31*, 32
Guangxi province, 6, *21*
Guangxu emperor, 37
Guangzhou, 6, *6*, *7*

hairstyles, 2, 28, 30, 32
'half dress', 25, *26*
Hakka, 32
Han Chinese, 19, 43, 46
    dress, 19
    pattern, 46
    symbolism, 36, 46
Han Chinese women, 30, *31*
    clothing, non-official, 30, 31, *31*
Han dynasty, 53
Hanlin Academy, 9, 11, *12*
headwear, 36
    graduation hat, 6
    Manchu woman's headdress, 30, *30*, 32
    mandarin's summer hat, *26*, 28
    mandarin's winter hat, 22, *26*, 28
Hong Kong, 6, 14, *27*, 39

Illustrated Catalogue of Ritual Paraphernalia of the Qing Dynasty, 19, 35
Imperial Army, 1
Imperial Chancery, 11
imperial family, 1, 2, 20, 21, 33, 47
imperial insignia, 33, 34, 35, 37, 47, 48, 58

insignia badges, 33, 34, 35, 38, 53; *see also* badges of rank
Inner Mongolia, 2

jinshi, see graduate, metropolitan
junxiu, see student
juren, see graduate, provincial

Kangxi Encyclopaedia, 47
key-fret pattern, 36, 57

leopard, 43, 45, 60
lion, 43, 45, 60
lishui, 23, 36, 39, 47, 60
long life symbols, 33, 36, 37, 47, 47, 48; *see also shou, wan*

magua, 26, *27*, 60; *see also* riding jacket
Manchu, 1, 3, 19, 32
    army, 13, 43
    bannermen, 1, 13, 43
    costume, 2, 19, 23, 29, 35, 36, 46
    empire, 2
    language, 2, 19
Manchu women, 29
    non-official clothing, 29, *30*
    official clothing, 29
Manchuria, 1, 2
mandarin, 3, 11, 13, 17, 18, 28
    civil, 3, 11, 15, 29
    dress, 19, 20, 21; *see also* clothing, official and non-official
    duties, 11
    military, 3, 11, 14, 15, 29
    ranks of, 11, 14, *16*, 24, 40
    regulations of, 15
    salary of, 14, 15, *16*
    square, *see* badges of rank
mandarin chain, 29
mandarin duck, 40, 41, 60
military commander-in-chief, 14, 60
Ming dynasty, 1, 3, 13, 20, 33, 38, 40, 53
Mongols, 13, 33
mountain motif, 23, 38, 47

New Territories, 6, 39
nietai, see provincial judge
noblemen, 1
    insignia, 33, 34, 36, 38, 42, 45, 47
    robes, 21, 33
see also imperial family

oriole, 38, 40, 42, 60
Outer Mongolia, 2

panther, 43, 45, 60
paradise flycatcher, 40, 42, 60
peacock, 40, 41, 60
peacock feather plume, *12*, *22*, 28, 29
Peking knot, *see* embroidery stitches
phoenix, 34, 47
provincial judge, 13, *16*, 60
pufu, *see* surcoat
purchase of degrees and ranks, 3, 9, 11, *12*, 36, 43, 60
puzi, *see* badges of rank

Qianlong emperor, 19, 35, 47
qifu, *see* dragon robe
qilin, 34, 43, 45, 60
Qin dynasty, 1
quail, 40, 41, 60

Reform period, 37
Republic of China, 32, 38
rhinoceros, 43, *44*, 45, 60
riding jacket, 19, 35,
roundels, 33, 35, 36, 37, 47; *see also* badges of rank

satin, 24, 28, 30, 53
sea horse, 43, *44*, 45, 60
Shandong province, 28
Shang dynasty, 48, 55
shoes, 30, 32
shou symbol, 34, 36, 37, 38, 48, 57, 60
Shunzhi emperor, 1
Sichuan, 28
silk, 20, 24, 25, 26, 38, 53
gauze, 24, 53, 57
silver pheasant, 40, 41, 60
Six Boards, the, 11
skirt, 31

sleeveless vest, Han Chinese woman's, 31
Manchu woman's, 29, 30, *30*
Song dynasty, 33, 53
student, 5, 8, 9, 60
government, 5, 60
military government, 10, 60
surcoat, 22, *22*, 24, *25*, 26, 35, 38, 60
sun disk, 35, 59
swastika pattern, 48, 60
symbols, 23, 24, 34, 35, 36, 37, 46, 47, *56*

Taiwan, 2
Tang dynasty, 3
thunder line pattern, 48
Tibet, 2, 59
tidu, *see* military commander-in-chief
tiger, 43, 45, 60
trousers, 31
Turkestan, 2

viceroy, 11, 13, 14, 15, 17, 60; *see also* governor-general
Victoria and Albert Museum, 29

wan symbol, *see* swastika pattern
Wanli reign, 33
wife of mandarin, *18*, 29; *see also* Han Chinese and Manchu women
wild goose, 40, 41, 60

xiezhi, 42, 60
Xinjiang, 2
xiucai, *see* student , government

yamen, 6, 14, 17, 18
Yangzhou, 53
Yuan dynasty, 53

zhitai, *see* viceroy
Zhou dynasty, 3